SAVED ʙʏ THE DOG

Unleashing Potential with Psychiatric Service Dogs

Anne Martinez

Saved by the Dog: Unleashing Potential with Psychiatric Service Dogs

Published by Anventure LLC 1008 Woodland Pointe Dr., Kernersville, NC 27284 USA.

This publication is designed to provide accurate and authoritative information in regard to the subject matter covered. It is sold with the understanding that the publisher is not engaged in rendering legal, accounting, or other professional service. If legal advice or other expert services are required, the services of a competent professional should be sought.

While every precaution has been taken in the creation of this book, the publisher and author assume no responsibility for errors or omissions, or for damages resulting from the use of the information contained herein.

Website URL: http://servicedogspot.com

Cover photo by Brittany Rogers

First Edition

ISBN: 978-0-9984636-0-5

To Tonya and Rebecca Hart of Harts2Paws for giving me the incredible gift of Maisy.

Table of Contents

Acknowledgements...xi

Introduction 1

Chapter 1: Just the Facts.. 3

    Qualifying for a Service Dog 6

        Meeting the Disability Qualification 8

        Meeting the Training Requirement 9

    Recognizing Other Types of Assistance Dogs............................ 11

    Where Service Dogs Come From... 13

    Understanding the Commitment... 15

    What if I Don't Qualify? 16

Chapter 2: Personal Stories...17

    Kelly and Isaac.. 17

    Michael and BoBo... 20

    Lindsay and Grace.. 22

Chapter 3: Is a Service Dog Right for You?........................25

    Understanding Service Dog Interventions................................. 27

        Useful PSD Behaviors 27

            Hey, stop that!...28

            Excuse me, did you know… 28

            Bringing you back to the here and now 29

            Smoothing rough moments...29

        Working with Symptoms..30

            Anxiety & Panic 30

            Crowd Anxiety/Agoraphobia..31

            Depression or Sadness 32

            Dissociation or Fear Paralysis 32

            Fear of Intruders..32

            Hallucinations..33

            Impaired Memory & Concentration 33

            Medication Side Effects..33

            Night Terrors/Nightmares 34

Racing Thoughts 35

Repetitive /Compulsive Behaviors 35

Self-harm 35

Sensory Overload 36

Suicidal Ideation 36

Service Dogs are not Robots 37

Three-Way Service Dog Teams 38

Developing a Personal Task List **39**

Considering Social Implications...............................**41**

Factoring in Friends and Family 41

Employment Matters...43

Managing Public Encounters..43

Chapter 4: Obtaining a Service Dog from a Program **45**

Finding and Evaluating Service Dog Programs....................**48**

Getting Organized 48

Finding Service Dog Providers...50

Assessing a Service Dog Organization................................50

Understanding the Application Process **52**

Questions You Must Ask 56

Questions You Must Answer..58

Submitting Applications...**59**

Chapter 5: Deciding to Owner-Train...**61**

Previewing the Journey **62**

Before you Begin **64**

Recognizing Owner Training Myths 65

Are You Dog Ready?...66

What is Your Washout Plan? 67

Sources for a Service Dog Prospect **68**

Puppy vs. Adult Prospect 69

The Started Dog Option 70

Selecting "The One" **70**

Identifying Suitable Breeds 71

Considering Size 71

Factoring in Activity Level...72

Trainability is Key..72

Coat Type Concerns..72

Social Considerations 73

Mixed Breeds and Mutts 74

Need Help? There's an App for That! 74

Health Issues to Check Up On 75

Testing for Temperament 75

Commonly Used Assessments..............................77

Do-it-Yourself Temperament Testing......................79

Developing a Training Agenda...................... **82**

Shaping Up Social Skills......................................85

Laying Obedience Foundations............................86

Minding Service Dog Manners.............................87

Practicing Public Access Skills 88

Individualized Work & Task Training......................89

Linking Up with a Trainer **89**

Keeping a Training Log **90**

Graduating to Full Service Dog Status.......... **92**

Chapter 6: Working with a Professional Trainer...... **95**

Recognizing Training Styles **97**

Considering Education and Certifications............ **100**

Assessing Professional Experience.................. **101**

Contract Matters **101**

Selecting a Training Format.......................... **103**

Group Classes...103

Private Lessons...104

Board & Train..104

Chapter 7: Knowing Service Dog Laws **107**

No Certification or Registration Required **109**

The Americans with Disabilities Act.................... **110**

Qualifying to Have a Service Animal 111

Defining Disability..111

Defining Service Dog 113

Public Access Rights 114

The Two Questions...115

Exclusions and Special Cases 116

Section 504 of the Rehabilitation Act of 1973 .... **117**

Taking a Service Dog to School 118

Taking a Service Dog to Work 118

State Service Dog Laws 120

Obtaining a Housing Accommodation 120

Flying with a Service Dog or SDiT 124

Reporting a Violation of Your Rights 126

Tax Breaks for Service Dog Expenses....................................128

Chapter 8: Getting to Know the Service Dog Community *131*

Service Dogs on Social Media..132
  Joining Facebook Groups 132
  Learning by Example on YouTube..134
  Following Service Dog Teams on Instagram 135

Benefitting from Bloggers 135

Service Dog Organizations 136
  Psychiatric Service Dog Partners (PSDP)...136
  International Association of Assistance Dog Partners (IAADP)........137
  Assistance Dogs International (ADI)..138
  Service Dog Central...139

Resources for Answering Legal Questions 139
  Job Accommodation Network (JAN) 139
  Animal Legal & Historical Center 140
  ADA Information Line...140

Chapter 9: Social Skills for Dogs & Handlers *141*

Practicing Service Dog Etiquette 143

Socializing Your Dog 144

Deflecting Unwanted Interest..146
  Putting Body Language to Work 147
  Practicing Speaking (Really) 148
  Handing Out Information Cards...149
  Equipping Your Dog 151
    Dressing for Success 151
    Handy Commands for Evading Pushy People..........................153
  Dealing with Drive-bys 153

Handling an Access Challenge 154

Working the Process 155
If Working the Process Doesn't Work..156

Being a Service Dog Advocate **158**

Playing Service Dog Bingo **159**

Chapter 10: Out and About with Your Service Dog **161**

Everyday Encounters **162**
Navigating Escalators, Elevators & Stairs..162
Utilizing Public Restrooms 165

Hitting the Road (or the Friendly Skies) **165**
Travelling by Air 166
Before You Leave Home 166
What to Expect from Airport Security 168
Boarding the Plane & During the Flight..168
Taking a Taxi, Train, or Bus 169
Travelling by Car 170
Staying in a Hotel or Motel 172

Tending to Medical Care **173**
Medical Appointments 173
Hospitals, Emergency Rooms & Ambulances 174

Attending Recreational & Social Activities **176**
Dining Out 176
Taking in a Movie 177
Going to Church 178
Working Out at the Gym..178
Hiking and Camping 178
Amusement Parks & Resorts 180

Chapter 11: Peering into the Future **183**

Peeking Inside the Canine Mind **184**

Sniffing Out Stress **185**

Wearable Computing for Service Dogs...................................... **186**

Studying Service Dogs for PTSD **186**

Changing Legislation **188**

Appendix A: Federal FAQs **193**

ADA Revised Requirements: Service Animals............................. **194**

Frequently Asked Questions about Service Animals and the ADA 199

Appendix B: Sample Letters *211*

PSD Housing Accommodation Request Letter from a Person with a Disability..212

SDiT Housing Accommodation Request Letter from a Person with a Disability 213

PSD Housing Accommodation Request Letter from a Medical Provider..214

SDiT/ESA Housing Accommodation Request Letter from a Medical Provider..215

PSD Flying Letter from a Medical Provider.............................216

ESA Flying Letter from a Medical Provider.............................216

PSD Workplace Accommodation Request from a Person with a Disability..218

PSD Workplace Accommodation Request Letter from a Medical Provider..219

Appendix C: Writing a Letter for a Service Dog or Emotional Support Animal: Tips for Medical Professionals.....................*221*

Appendix D: Fundraising Tips....................................*223*

Glossary *231*

Index..*239*

About the Author *245*

Acknowledgements

With gratitude to all who helped me bring this book to you:

- Kelly Morris for thoughtful, detailed technical editing.

- Lindsay Brown of Paws Then Play, LLC (pawsthenplay.com), for extensive consultation and education about dog training and behavior, and ongoing support throughout the writing of this book.

- Jessica Jolly of ALT-Enter, LLC (altentertraining.com), for providing critical assistance with the intricacies of Microsoft Word formatting and styling.

- Michael and Kara McDaniel, Lindsay Brown, and Kelly Morris for sharing their personal stories of working as part of a service dog team.

- Brittany Rogers, for providing the cover photo of service dogs belonging to members of the Service Animals of North Carolina (SANC) Facebook group.

- Christine San Jose for reviewing drafts and sharing her wise editorial guidance.

- Rebecca Martinez for proofreading.

- Tonya Hart of Harts2Paws for supporting this project from day one.

Introduction

Do you struggle with mental health issues? Or does someone you know? Perhaps for many years? Therapy and medication offer hope, but sometimes not enough. There's another option that many people are just beginning to learn about: psychiatric service dogs (PSDs). For many years, service dogs have been assisting people with disabilities such as blindness or mobility impairments; now they're helping people with serious mental health concerns as well.

PSDs can alleviate many of the incapacitating symptoms of disabling mental illnesses. They can interrupt panic and anxiety attacks, wake their handlers from nightmares, create physical space around their handlers in public places, and perform many more helpful tasks. Equally important to most people with mental health concerns, PSDs also provide the unconditional love and sense of security that dogs are known for. Quite simply, they help people return to greater participation in the world.

There is confusion along with the excitement about the possibilities of psychiatric service dogs. For example, psychiatric service dogs, emotional support animals, and therapy dogs serve different functions, and it's important to know the differences. Many PSDs are professionally trained by service dog organizations, but it's also possible (and legal) to train your own PSD. You might also be surprised to learn that having a PSD can actually cause more anxiety for some people than it alleviates, due to the public scrutiny and responsibilities that it generates.

In this book, you will learn all about PSDs, the wonders they can perform, and the drawbacks that accompany owning one. You'll find out how to actually obtain a PSD, and learn the pros and cons of going through a service dog provider versus owner training. You'll also get to know United States laws pertaining to service dogs in public, in housing, and when travelling. There's also plenty of advice for successfully navigating the world with a PSD at your side.

I wrote this book to enable you to make an informed choice about whether or not partnering with a psychiatric service dog is right for you, and if it is, to assist you through the process of becoming a successful service dog handler. I hope it helps you or someone you know.

Chapter 1

Just the Facts

In This Chapter

➤ Understanding who qualifies to have a service dog

➤ Learning the difference between service dogs, emotional support animals, and therapy dogs

➤ Finding out where service dogs come from

➤ Considering the challenges of life with a service dog at your side

➤ It doesn't have to be all or nothing...

If mental health issues are making it difficult or impossible for you to work, socialize, or maybe even go to the grocery store, you need help. You've probably already looked in the obvious places – a doctor, therapy, medication – but there's another option that may benefit you as much or more - the humble dog. Not just any dog, but a trained psychiatric service dog. A growing number of people who suffer from serious psychological conditions such as major depressive disorder, PTSD, bipolar disorder, OCD, and other mental health impairments are turning to canine helpers with life-altering results.

While there are many potential mental health benefits provided by the simple presence of a pet, a psychiatric service dog (PSD) is much more than a traditional companion animal. PSDs are trained to provide specific assistance to people in ways that alleviate or prevent distressing symptoms related to their condition. For a person with substantial mental health issues, partnership with a PSD can make a huge difference in quality of life.

For example, a PSD can interrupt panic attacks, provide calming pressure at times of distress, remind you to take your medicine, provide "crowd control" to make sure people stay out of your personal space in public, and/or call for help on a special K9 phone. They can help in other ways too. For example, if you constantly drop things due to medication-induced tremors, your dog could pick them up for you. A PSD can be trained to enter a room before you and turn on a light, fetch a family member if you need help, wake you up from nightmares, and much more. Not every dog does all these things, because not every person needs them; PSDs are individually trained to assist their owner's specific needs.

In addition to specific tasks that PSDs can perform to aid their owners, there are loads of "coincidentals" that come with having a canine companion in the house that can be especially beneficial to people struggling with mental health issues. These include increased incentive to exercise, decreased loneliness, and an increase in positive social interactions. In addition, numerous studies link pet ownership with health benefits such as reduced risk for heart disease and lower blood pressure.

The Americans with Disabilities Act (ADA) specifically includes psychiatric service dogs and protects the public access rights of those who need them. With few exceptions, a service dog can go wherever its handler goes – work, school, the grocery store, a restaurant, the emergency room.

That's great news, but it's not all rainbows and unicorns. There's a lot of incomplete, inaccurate, and downright fraudulent information floating around about service dogs and PSDs in particular. Finding out exactly what a PSD is, what one can and can't do, who is eligible to have one, and where you might actually get one can be more challenging than buttering toast with your nose. While a game changer for some, service dogs are not a magic answer for everyone, and there's a lot more involved than is immediately apparent. If you go online and google "service dog" here's what will happen:

1) Solicitations offering to register your dog as a service dog will cascade across the top of your screen - which is incredibly deceptive on multiple levels. First of all, the certificate and/or ID you buy from such places has absolutely zero legal meaning. You can't transform any dog into a service dog by registering it in a database somewhere; there are specific legal requirements defining what a service dog is and who can have one and registration is not currently one of them, at least not in the United States. Representing your dog as a service dog when it's not is illegal! It would appear, however, that offering to sell anyone and everyone a certificate and "service dog ID" is not.

2) A litany of stories about "fake service dogs" will come next - see #1 above. Some people do this knowingly, deliberately "playing the system" without understanding the potential consequences, but others are simply operating under incorrect information that they probably found online. The stories about fake service dogs often include misinformation themselves; even the reporters are confused.

Wouldn't you like to know if a psychiatric service dog is an appropriate idea for YOU without having to wade through reams of bad or misleading advice? Even online service dog communities have well-meaning but erroneous information mixed in with the good stuff you really need to know. That's why this book exists.

Psychiatric service dogs? Really?

The phrase "service dog" most quickly summons up an image of a guide dog for the blind, or perhaps as a helper for a person who uses a wheelchair. The concept of service dogs to assist people with psychological disorders didn't really receive serious attention until military veterans suffering from post-traumatic stress disorder (PTSD) began to be paired with them, with life-restoring results.

I'm not talking about that feel-good sensation you get when Fido snuggles up with you on the couch after a bad day - though the power of that should not be underestimated - these dogs are trained in specific tasks directly related to easing the symptoms of PTSD.

In 2011, veteran Luis Carlos Montalván told his story in a book, *Until Tuesday: A Wounded Warrior and the Golden Retriever Who Saved Him*. Montalván (www.luiscarlosmontalvan.com), a 17-year veteran and retired Captain of the U.S. Army, suffered life-altering injuries during his service. By his account, among the most crippling was a psychiatric wound - post-traumatic stress disorder (PTSD), a disability that's largely invisible and often unrecognized. PTSD is now known to be a condition that that can have devastating consequences, leading to misery, isolation, and even suicide. Montalván recounts how he was headed straight down that dark path when a four-legged miracle intervened, in the form of a service dog named Tuesday.

Tuesday came into Montalván's life through a service dog program, East Coast Assistance Dogs (ECAD). Tuesday assisted both physically and psychologically, but it's the psychological help that is at the core of this amazing story, and it is the bond that developed between them that Montalván credits with restoring his life. The PTSD hasn't gone away, but he became able to navigate the world despite it, with the assistance of Tuesday. He went on to graduate from the Columbia School of Journalism and become a major advocate of service dogs for both visible and invisible disabilities.

The publication of *Until Tuesday* was a milestone in the history of psychiatric service dogs. In addition to bringing an emotional story of healing to readers and explaining very specifically how an assistance dog can provide assistance, it also revealed the challenges of navigating the world with a service dog at your side. Time and again business owners, bus drivers, and others refused to accept that Tuesday was a service dog because the only service dogs they'd ever heard of were those that guide the blind. This unfortunately still occurs today, but significantly less so thanks to the efforts of Montalván and other service dog advocates.

Qualifying for a Service Dog

Because service dogs are considered medically necessary for their handlers, handlers are permitted to bring them places traditional pets are not allowed. To keep just anyone from calling their dog a service dog so they can take advantage of this, many countries have specific legislation defining what qualifies a dog as a service dog and detailing legal protections accorded to service dogs and their handlers. These spell out regulations regarding things like public access, housing rights, and traveling by air with a service dog.

These legal rights are accorded to the person using the dog, not to the dog itself.

In the United States, to legally qualify to have a service dog (psychiatric or otherwise), you must meet two criteria:

1) **You must have a disability.** The definition of disability is specified in the Americans with Disabilities Act (ADA). Mental health conditions are specifically included.

2) **The dog must be individually trained to do work or perform tasks for you that are directly related to your disability.** The specific type of training the dog has is very relevant to meeting this requirement.

That's it. Don't be fooled by websites that offer to sell you registration or certification that "makes" your pet a service dog. There is no such thing. If you're disabled, including by a mental illness, and your dog is trained to do things that mitigate your disability, then per the Americans with Disabilities Act (ADA), you qualify.

The ADA isn't the only legislation that affects service dog handlers, but it's the one that defines the over-riding standard for the legal definition of a service dog team for the most purposes. It sets the rules surrounding public access and workplace requirements.

The ADA is federal legislation that applies across the entire country. It requires businesses, state and local government agencies, and nonprofit organizations that provide good or services to the public to make "reasonable modifications" to their operations when necessary to accommodate persons with disabilities. As part of this, it specifically states that these entities, even if they have a "no pets" policy, must allow service animals into their facilities.

Additional laws regulate flying with a "service animal" (Air Carrier Access Act) and housing rights for people with an "assistance animal" (Fair Housing Act). Chapter 7: Knowing Service Dog Laws details specific rights and the laws that provide them.

Meeting the Disability Qualification

You fit the legal definition of having a disability under the ADA if:

- ✓ you have a physical or mental impairment that substantially limits one or more major life activities

  or

- ✓ you have a record of such an impairment

There's no comprehensive checklist of conditions to refer to, but the ADA regulations do provide a definition of what qualifies as a *"physical or mental impairment"*:

- ✓ any physiological disorder or condition, cosmetic disfigurement, or anatomical loss affecting one or more body systems, such as neurological, musculoskeletal, special sense organs, respiratory (including speech organs), cardiovascular, reproductive, digestive, genitourinary, immune, circulatory, hemic, lymphatic, skin, and endocrine.

- ✓ any mental or psychological disorder, such as intellectual disability (formerly termed mental retardation), organic brain syndrome, emotional or mental illness, and specific learning disabilities.

Not all impairments are considered disabilities. For example, a short temper or a tendency toward anxiety or other individual personality traits not linked to a psychological disorder are not considered disabilities, even though they might make your life difficult.

How bad does the impairment have to be to be considered *substantially limiting*? It must be substantial as compared to most people in the general population, but it is NOT required that you cannot perform the activity at all or even are severely restricted from doing so. Simply having a diagnosis of a particular condition does not automatically qualify you as disabled under the ADA.

If your impairment is episodic and comes and goes, which of course is often true of psychological disorders such as major depressive disorder, bipolar disorder, and schizophrenia, it still counts if it substantially limits a major life activity when it's active.

At this point, you might be wondering what is considered as a *major life activity*. ADA regulations provide examples to help us:

> "caring for oneself, performing manual tasks, seeing, hearing, eating, sleeping, walking, standing, sitting, reaching, lifting, bending, speaking, breathing, learning, reading, concentrating, thinking, communicating, interacting with others, and working."

Although that's a pretty long list, it's not considered exhaustive. If it came down to a lawsuit, other activities might qualify as well.

Of particular interest to potential psychiatric service dog teams, a government FAQ provides guidance on "specific impairments that will be easily concluded to substantially limit a major life activity," and the list includes: major depressive disorder, bipolar disorder, post-traumatic stress disorder, obsessive-compulsive disorder, and schizophrenia.

You don't need a formal diagnosis from a physician or medical professional to be considered disabled under the ADA. You may, however, need documentation for certain purposes, such as requesting a reasonable accommodation at work, living in no-pets housing, or flying with a service animal. These situations and the relevant laws are discussed in detail in Chapter 7: Knowing Service Dog Laws

Meeting the Training Requirement

A service dog team has two parts: a handler with a disability and a dog that is trained specifically to assist with that disability. A dog whose sole duty is to make you feel comforted simply by its presence does not count - even if that dog has a perfect heel, comes instantly when you call, and would never even contemplate chewing anything but its own toys. That would still be a wonderful dog, but it would not qualify as a service dog under the ADA.

To rise to the level of service dog, the dog must be trained to take a specific action when needed to assist with a disability. Most service dogs are trained to perform multiple assistance behaviors but legally only one is required.

The ADA defines a service animal as:

1) A dog that has been individually trained to do work or perform tasks for an individual with a disability.

2) The task(s) performed by the dog must be directly related to the person's disability.

This is why simply providing comfort through being at your side, as helpful as it might be, does not count - because it's a natural dog thing, not something the dog was specifically trained to do as needed for a disability.

For a behavior to be considered trained, the dog must reliably do it on cue. That cue might be something you say, a hand signal, or body language the dog is trained to pick up on, or in some cases even the time of day.

For example, if you suffer from anxiety attacks related to your disability, and the dog is trained to detect your personal signals of rising anxiety (perhaps hyperventilating or jiggling legs) and respond with a specific action (such as pressure therapy) that prevents or lessens a full-blown anxiety attack, that's considered a service dog task and legally qualifies the animal as a service dog.

The trained task, pressure therapy, is directly related to the disability that the handler has and thus the dog meets both of the criteria. A dog that meets the training qualification for one person would not necessarily qualify when paired with a different handler with a different disability.

There are, in fact, many qualifying service dog tasks that are extremely helpful to people struggling with psychological disorders. Reminding you to take your medication counts, as does blocking people from coming too close, waking you up if you're too drowsy from medication side effects to respond to an alarm clock, and others which you can learn about in Chapter 3: Is a Service Dog Right for You?

In case you're wondering who is going to do all this training, the answer is that it could be a professional trainer or it could be you. Practically speaking, it's often a combination. Legally speaking, the ADA specifically states that people with disabilities have the right to train the dog themselves and are not required to use a professional dog training program.

It's important to understand that some states have their own regulations regarding service dogs, but here's the thing: whichever is less restrictive trumps the other. So essentially federal law sets the rules, and if a state wants to be more permissive with service dogs, they can, but they cannot be more restrictive.

Recognizing Other Types of Assistance Dogs

Many people use the terms service dog, therapy dog, and emotional support animal interchangeably; however, other than being warm, furry, and four-legged they are quite different things, both legally and functionally. They're all canine assistants, but they do different jobs. If you refer to someone's service dog as their "therapy dog," they might not bother to correct you, but you can bet they'll notice. Therapy dogs and emotional support animals aren't covered under the same laws and their handlers don't receive the same special access rights that service dog handlers do. You may also run across the term "companion dog," but that refers to a pet (though potentially well-trained) and isn't a type of assistance dog.

A *therapy dog* provides affection and comfort to people, other than its owner, who need it. Often they go with their owners on a volunteer basis to settings such as hospitals, retirement homes, schools, or perhaps a disaster relief area. Some therapy dogs participate in formal animal-assisted therapy settings, where they help take part in physical or occupational therapy programs at a rehabilitation center or reside at a care facility and are handled by trained staff members. They must be well-tempered and affectionate, calm in all situations, and must be socialized to many environments, including places with canes, wheelchairs, children, loud noises, and different floor surfaces. Many therapy dog teams obtain certification through recognized program in order to demonstrate their suitability and as a way to obtain liability insurance.

An *emotional support animal* (ESA) provides therapeutic benefit to its owner who has a mental or psychiatric disability through providing companionship. Usually an ESA is either a dog or a cat, but other animals can qualify, leading at times to bizarre stories of miniature pot-bellied pigs on airplanes. The person with the ESA must have a verifiable disability, but no training or certification is required for the animal.

The primary advantage of having an animal classified as an ESA is to receive special treatment in housing and travel. Under the federal Fair Housing Act (FHAct), an ESA is considered a "reasonable accommodation" in housing that has a "no pets" rule and must be allowed. Through the Air Carrier Access Act, ESAs are also permitted to accompany their owners on plane trips without extra charge. ESAs don't have public access rights or legal protections accorded to service dogs. Table 1-1 summarizes the differences between types of assistance dogs.

Table 1-1: Roles & Rights of Assistance Dogs in the USA

	Service Dog	*Emotional Support Dog*	*Therapy Dog*
Handler must have a disability	☑	☑	
Specially trained to do tasks or work related to handler's disability	☑		

	Service Dog	Emotional Support Dog	Therapy Dog
Allowed to accompany handler to public places such as restaurants, stores, hotels	☑		
Allowed to live in "no pets" housing	☑	☑	
Allowed to travel on airplanes with owner	☑	☑	
Helps owner	☑	☑	
Helps others			☑

Where Service Dogs Come From

It would be nice if you (or your doctor) could just ring up your health insurance company, notify them you qualify for and want a service dog, and sit back and wait for the pitter-patter of paws at your front door. Of course it doesn't actually work that way. This is a partnership you're probably going to have to go through a lot of effort to make happen. Health insurance isn't going to pitch in, and there's a growing demand for psychiatric service dogs but nothing approaching a matching supply.

A service dog has to master all the usual obedience stuff, but at graduate level, and then get a doctorate in how to serve their eventual handler. Anywhere along the training, the dog may "wash out" from service dog training and be re-homed as an over-achieving household pet or emotional support animal.

On top of this, the majority of dogs don't have an appropriate temperament for service dog work. It's not all uncommon for even carefully selected dogs to wash out of training somewhere along the way. They might grow up to be fearful of children, loud noises, or busy places, be unable to resist chasing squirrels, or simply turn out to be not as trainable as originally estimated. In rare cases, a physical deterrent like a joint condition might pop up.

Although a service dog does not have to be born into the job from puppyhood, that's where many start. From there, depending on the dog and on the handler's needs, it's about a 2-year journey to fully trained, public-access-ready service dog. An adult dog that enters service dog training could become ready more quickly as it (hopefully) has maturity on its side and preliminaries such as potty training nailed down.

There are basically two sources for these highly educated, canine miracle-workers:

1) **A service dog program** - You apply to a program, which trains the dog for you. Most often the dog is selected and provided by the program, but some programs will train a client's existing dog, if that dog is one of the rare few with an appropriate temperament and characteristics. There are both nonprofit and for-profit service dog programs. A lucky few individuals, mostly military veterans, can get hooked up with a dog at no charge. However, many programs charge $10,000 or even much more. This isn't entirely unreasonable given what it takes to raise and train a service dog. There is often a 1-2 year wait (or longer) between being accepted to the program and receiving a dog. Many people seeking a psychiatric service dog will find it very difficult to find a program that will accept them and that they can afford, but for some people this is the only realistic route anyway.

2) **Owner trained** - You obtain an appropriate candidate dog from a breeder or rescue. You train the dog with the help of a professional trainer when possible and your own determination when not. The training process will still take 1-2 years but the dog will be with you, bonding to you, and being a companion during that time. The total cost depends

on where you get the dog and how much professional training you enlist. It can still be substantial; it's just spread out over much greater time. In addition, many dogs start owner training but fail to finish successfully, despite investments of time, money, and hope. Although it's not easy, it can be done, and people do it all the time.

Each of these options has pros and cons, which are explored in greater detail in Chapter 4: Obtaining a Service Dog from a Program and Chapter 5: Deciding to Owner Train.

Understanding the Commitment

By now you probably have a sense of the life-changing help a PSD can provide, but doubtless you're also realizing that, like most things in life, they are a blessing that also comes with complications. As wonderful as service dogs can be, they do require a lot of work and no small amount of financial expense. Having a service dog is a lot like having a young child; you take it virtually everywhere with you, clean up after it, pay its bills, and deal with its foibles. A service dog is not a robot and won't always perform flawlessly.

A service dog requires ongoing training. Tasks that aren't used regularly, such as responding to a fire alarm, must be practiced regularly for the life of the dog or they will be forgotten. You must tend to its health, mind its weight, diet and exercise, and adhere to protocols that were laid out during training. You must understand that it's a dog, and a working dog on top of that, and interact with it from that perspective, not expect it to behave like a human. It sounds obvious, but a startling number of potential service dog owners seem to expect otherwise.

There's another thing you should know. When you go out with a service dog, people stare at you and ask intrusive personal questions. It happens to all service dog handlers, and escalates when your disability is invisible to casual appraisal. Most people are just curious, but even that gets old faster than unwrapped cheese. Others will look at you, see you're not blind or in a wheelchair, and give you an accusatory eye, as might happen to someone who gets out of a car parked in a handicapped spot and appears normal externally, but in reality desperately needs that spot because they can't walk 10 steps without getting out of breath. This is simple ignorance, as you don't have to be a walking basket case to have a service dog, but it's stressful nonetheless. Still, most service dog owners find the benefits are well worth it, and the public reception of service dogs of all kinds seems to be improving everyday as people become more accustomed to their presence. Personal questions are usually just a reflection of interest, opening an opportunity to educate and enlighten people about service dogs.

What if I Don't Qualify?

If your mental health problems don't rise to the level of a disability, you don't legally qualify to have a psychiatric service dog. If you have a physical disability, you may qualify that way and cross-train your service dog in psychiatric tasks.

If you still don't qualify to be part of a legally-protected service dog team, please don't write off the idea of canine mental health rescue immediately. You can gain many of the same benefits by training a carefully chosen dog to perform psychiatric service dog tasks anyway. Your dog won't automatically be able to go to the grocery store or to workplace or ride a bus with you, or receive other special access accorded to service dog teams, but it can still create a transformational change in your daily life. Perhaps such a dog might even be the mojo that keeps your issues from rising to the level of becoming a disability. Wouldn't that be something?

Chapter 2

Personal Stories

In This Chapter

➢ Tales from the trenches

I t's difficult to get the true measure of what it might mean to partner with a psychiatric service dog until you've done it. At the same time, it's important to get a solid idea of what's possible and realistic before diving in. Perhaps the best way to address this conundrum is to ask those who've pioneered the way; people who are already part of working PSD teams are uniquely positioned to describe what you can expect. In this chapter, you'll meet three of them:

✓ Kelly and Isaac, from Ohio

✓ Michael and BoBo, from North Carolina

✓ Lindsay and Grace, from North Carolina

Kelly and Michael obtained their canine partners through service dog providers. Lindsay owner trained Grace. These handlers have experienced the joys and challenges of teaming up with a psychiatric service dog, and they're willing to share.

Kelly and Isaac

Kelly and Isaac live in rural north-central Ohio. They've been a team for four years. Kelly, who is 45 years old, has had post-traumatic stress disorder (PTSD) for many years, due to childhood trauma. That's the primary reason she wanted a psychiatric service dog (PSD). "I'd been in treatment for PTSD for a long time, done lots of therapy, was on pretty effective meds, but I was still very disabled," Kelly says. "There were things that therapy and medication could not do for me that I thought a service dog (SD) could do."

Kelly researched her options. She did a lot of reading, chatted with other service dog handlers online, talked to her doctor about it, and came to the conclusion that a PSD would likely be a good solution for her. But where to get one?

After further research and much thought, Kelly decided her best option was to obtain a dog from a service dog program rather than attempt to owner train. "I considered owner training but had no experience with dogs. I'm glad I didn't try to owner train because I think with my severe anxiety, I would have found it very difficult and it probably would have ended up making my anxiety worse." Kelly explains. She feels that a lot of people underestimate the difficulty of owner training. "I do know people that have done a fantastic job owner training. But unfortunately I see a lot of people saying they want to train their own SD and they can't afford to hire a trainer and can someone please just tell them how to teach their dog to sit. And I always think if you don't even have any idea how to teach your dog to sit, how are you going to train an SD all by yourself?"

She found K9's in Special Service (K.I.S.S.) just a few hours from her home, applied to them, and was accepted. "It's a really small program and they are able and willing to really customize things to each person," Kelly says. "The dogs stay with puppy raisers or other volunteers for a while and learn basic manners and stuff, then they go to a trainer. The dog lives in the home of the trainer. The dog might spend some time with one trainer, then spend some time with another. The director of the program does a lot of the public access training herself. The trainer that did most of Isaac's training, and whom he lived with for more than a year, does a lot of the task training," she explains.

Although Kelly was prepared to wait, the process went relatively quickly. To pay for the PSD (she didn't know it would be Isaac until later), Kelly turned to fundraising, and in particular to local churches. With the generous help of her local community, she was able to raise the funds to cover the initial cost of acquiring a service dog. Within a year, she was called to meet Isaac, a 2-year-old yellow lab who came from a lab rescue program.

Team training followed a few months afterward. Kelly was a little anxious about the team training process, but it went very smoothly. "I would have a very hard time doing the kind of team training many programs do, with a packed schedule for a whole two weeks. I'd be exhausted and overwhelmed by the end of day two. But they were able to schedule things in a way that I could tolerate easily, with lots of breaks," she says.

Isaac performs many useful tasks for Kelly, such as turning on lights before Kelly enters a room. "Before getting Isaac, there were times I could not go to the bathroom all night because I couldn't walk into a dark bathroom," she reports. He also retrieves anxiety meds on command and also does it without being told if she begins to show early signs of an anxiety attack. "I will start to rock back and forth and he gets my meds and brings them to me and drops them in my lap, which reminds me to take them. I usually remember to take my meds myself but when I am very anxious, I do not think clearly and need to be reminded. Taking my medication at the beginning of an anxiety attack almost always prevents a lengthy and debilitating anxiety attack." In addition, Isaac interrupts compulsive skin picking, which Kelly sometimes does without realizing it.

Kelly also uses his blocking tasks, but not as much as she originally expected to. "He is trained to block in order to provide space for me in crowds, although I don't use that task often because I have found I feel better when he is where I can easily see him. I don't want him behind me. I guess he still provides space if people are too close in front or on the side, but part of my initial thinking was to have him 'watch my back' or something like that."

Isaac performs deep pressure therapy (DPT) as well, though not as much as Kelly would like. "I wish he did it more or was better at it. He is not cuddly. He does it, but usually only briefly."

Isaac helps alleviate some of Kelly's physical issues as well. He picks things up off the floor and gets clothes out of the dryer, activities that are painful for Kelly due to back problems and fibromyalgia.

All of this help doesn't come without some extra work on Kelly's part. "It's a lot of work, caring for a dog. Taking him out to pee at 6 am in winter in the snow when I am in a lot of pain is not easy or enjoyable. Also, there are days the attention I get in public with a SD really wears on me. I live in an area where SDs are not common and while access disputes are very rare here (most people are friendly and like dogs and mean well), drive by petting and personal questions and staring and distracting the dog are all extremely common."

Having Isaac is well worth the effort and expense though, Kelly reports. "I'm able to be more active than I used to be. I'm more independent, able to function better. I have less pain. Far fewer debilitating anxiety attacks, although I still do feel anxious at times. My physical and mental health have improved since getting Isaac."

Before Isaac, Kelly didn't like to go places by herself very often. In particular, going to medical appointments, especially things like gynecological checkups or dental work, was so stressful Kelly could only do it if a she could find a friend willing to accompany her. "It's not like I have a long list of friends that want to come to the gynecologist with me," Kelly says. But now Isaac is her companion for such things. He performs DPT before and after the appointment and interrupts nervous skin picking, making it possible for Kelly to go to appointments on her own. Well, not completely on her own, because these days, wherever Kelly goes, Isaac goes.

Michael and BoBo

Michael is a U.S. Navy veteran. He served from 2006-2013 in Djibouti, Comoros, and Kuwait. When he returned home, post-traumatic stress disorder (PTSD) and a traumatic brain injury (TBI) came with him. Michael needs someone with him most of the time, and until 8 months ago, his wife, Kara, filled that role on her own. Now, however, a 2-year-old golden retriever named BoBo has brought new freedom to both Michael and Kara. Before BoBo,

Michael couldn't go to the grocery store without having a flashback or needing to leave. Now, with BoBo at his side, Michael goes places all the time.

A nurse practitioner at Michael's primary care provider (outside the Veterans Administration) was the first to suggest that Michael might benefit from a service dog. She directed the family to Patriot Rovers, a High Point, NC, nonprofit organization that provides service dogs to veterans at no cost. Michael and his wife checked out the group and really liked what they saw. Michael applied to the program in June 2015. In October 2015, he was matched with BoBo. "I remember the day we found out like it was yesterday. It was truly one of the best days ever!" says Kara.

Bobo can do lots of things that help Michael. In public, he'll form a physical barrier between Michael and strangers, creating a feeling of safety. If Michael is having a flashback or feeling anxiety, he can give BoBo the "paws up" command, and BoBo will put his paws on Michael's chest and lay his weight on him. His pressure and breathing help bring Michael back to the present and helps the anxiety fade. Bobo also interrupts Michael's nightmares by waking him up.

"BoBo has helped me slowly be able to go back out in the real world," Michael says. "Before him, I spent pretty much all of my time in the house not wanting to go outside or go anywhere until my wife got home from work. Having him makes me feel a positive presence around me, like having my best friend with me all day, every day, and he has my back no matter what."

Navigating the world with a service dog hasn't come without challenges, and the attention BoBo draws in public is one of the largest. "It's kind of funny, the dog is supposed to be with you and go unnoticed and not draw attention, but it seems like it does the exact opposite. Kids, especially, have dog radar," he says. "They can spot him from far away like a great white shark and a drop of human blood."

On a few occasions, people have tried to bar him from bringing BoBo into an establishment, but he was able to persuade them in just a few sentences by citing the American's with Disabilities Act (ADA) and maintaining his cool. "If things like that happen to you, don't make a big deal out of it," he advises. "Just go with the flow and have it taken care of. Don't go call all of the news agencies and blow up social media and destroy the place. That's just wrong."

BoBo and Michael are now inseparable. Bobo constantly comes to Michael's aid, all day, every day. "The other day I was not feeling well at all. My head was throbbing with pain, I was having terrible thoughts of how I could stop the pain. I was in the bedroom on the bed, legs thrashing around, crying because it hurt so badly. BoBo came jingling into the bedroom (his microchip tag and rabies tag jingle together like a cow bell) and jumped right on the bed and lay right on top of me. He pretty much was holding me down and was licking the crap out of my hands trying to keep me grounded and bring me back. And let me tell you, it worked. My wife was trying to get me to calm down but it just wouldn't happen. But when BoBo comes to the rescue, magical things happen."

Lindsay and Grace

Lindsay's service dog Grace is a 7-1/2-year-old German shepherd who was surrendered to a rescue organization twice for different reasons. Lindsay, a dog behaviorist, was assigned to "make Grace adoptable." Grace was 2 years old at the time, a rambunctious teenager in dog terms, who had proven too much to handle for her previous owners. Lindsay immediately set to work on teaching her manners and basic obedience, so that Grace could find a new home, one that she could keep forever.

At the time, Lindsay didn't have a service dog and didn't intend to get one. In her work as an animal behaviorist, she'd trained dogs to public access standards for other disabled handlers, so she knew quite a bit about them, including that they can help with invisible disabilities as well as visible ones, but she'd never really considered how a service dog might help her with her own medical issues.

Lindsay has a troubling medical condition that substantially affects her daily life. Its most disabling feature is severe, incapacitating abdominal cramps that strike without warning, effectively dropping her in her tracks. There she remains, in the grip of cramps, until the spasms abate. If she can get to her medicine, they ease much faster, but standing upright is often out of the question when an attack is in full swing. Because the attacks are so severe and unpredictable, Lindsay used to avoid going out unless she had someone to accompany her and provide help if one should strike. But that was before she and Grace became a team.

As Lindsay was fostering Grace and working on basic training, she began to realize that Grace was actually very trainable, and even though she never considered herself "a shepherd person," Grace was growing on her. One day it occurred to her that Grace could be trained to fetch the medicine during an attack and bring it to her, get the phone, and perform other tasks that would make life easier for Lindsay. As an experienced trainer, she knew that most dogs don't have the right "stuff" to become a service dog. She thought she might be a bit biased about Grace, having fallen for her canine charms, so she asked another professional dog trainer to assess Grace's suitability for service dog work. That professional reported that Grace was a good candidate for service work. Shortly after that, Lindsay formally adopted Grace and began working on service training in earnest.

Even though Lindsay has a long history of working with and training dogs, she took her time working with Grace. For a long time, Lindsay says, she worked Grace in her in-training vest so she didn't have to really admit she had a service dog for herself. She started venturing out more, feeling confident with Grace at her side. Eventually she realized she could handle it, and the in training patches came off.

It wasn't until after Grace was trained to fetch medicine or get the phone that her most amazing talent showed itself. It may have been manifesting all along but Lindsay didn't connect the dots right away, or perhaps it only occurred as Grace bonded ever more closely with Lindsay. That amazing talent is the ability to alert Lindsay that an attack is about to occur, before it happens, giving her time to sit down, take medicine, and potentially ward it off entirely. Talk about life changing!

Grace's alert began as her raking her paws across Lindsay's thighs. At first Lindsay thought Grace was misbehaving, but then she realized it happened just before an episode. So when Grace did this she would sit down, and Grace would fetch her medicine. Not being too fond of getting clawed across the legs, Lindsay worked to reshape the alert to a nose bump instead. It took longer than she originally expected, but eventually Grace replaced the clawing with nose bumping.

Although Grace's primary duty is to help with Lindsay's invisible physical disability, her duties have evolved to include responding to psychological issues as well. If Lindsay gets really nervous, Grace will create space around her by circling her. She can also lead Lindsay to an exit if she's feeling overloaded.

Grace doesn't go everywhere with Lindsay. "If I'm having a good day and someone else is driving, I sometimes don't bring her. I don't always have to have her with me, but it gives me the option to function independently because I can have Grace with me when I need to," says Lindsay.

Chapter 3

Is a Service Dog Right for You?

In This Chapter

➤ Exploring the kinds of things service dogs can do

➤ Service dog tasks to help with mental health symptoms

➤ Beginning your personal service dog "to-do" list

➤ Recognizing the social impact of owning a service dog

If you're going to invest your hope, heart and money into a service dog, do it with your eyes wide open. Psychiatric service dogs (PSDs) have been trained to assist people with many different types of serious psychiatric disorders, including post-traumatic stress disorder (PTSD), bipolar disorder, major depressive disorder, schizophrenia, obsessive-compulsive disorder (OCD), agoraphobia, and other major mental illnesses; however, they are neither a magic cure-all nor automatically a good solution for everyone. In fact, for some people, getting a service dog actually causes more stress and struggles than it relieves, and they end up regretting it. That's why you really do need to give the idea of a service dog careful and thorough consideration before taking the plunge. Give yourself a preliminary pre-screen by answering the following five questions:

1) **Does my disorder rise to the level of a disability?**
   The Americans with Disabilities Act (ADA), which is the
   primary defining legislation regarding the use of service
   dogs in the United States, defines disability as "a physical
   or mental impairment that substantially limits one or more
   major life activities." Only people who have a disability are
   eligible to have a service dog. The legal definition of
   disability is discussed in Chapter 7: Knowing Service Dog
   Laws.

2) **Am I prepared to "out" myself as having a
   disability by having a service dog at my side?** You
   may be surprised by how many people will question
   whether you "really" need a service dog, including family
   members and friends who might question the severity of
   your psychological disorder. They'll eventually get used to
   the idea, but it's common to encounter resistance along the
   way; after all, most people have never even heard of
   psychiatric service dogs before and have no idea how
   they're any different from pet dogs. At times people will
   stare at you or ask intrusive questions when you go out
   with your dog.

3) **Do I have the financial resources to pay for food,
   vet bills, training, and other expenses of owning a
   dog?** The total cost of dog ownership can vary greatly
   depending on the dog, the owner's preferences, and luck,
   but several reputable sources put the figure north of
   $20,000 over a dog's lifetime, or an average of about
   $1,600 per year. That doesn't include any training.

4) **Am I able to meet a dog's needs for exercise,
   mental stimulation, love, and attention?** Family
   members and dog walkers can be enlisted to help, but the
   primary and ultimate responsibility will be yours. The good
   news is the dog is going to reciprocate by supplying you
   with these very things in return!

5) **Am I willing to dedicate myself to sticking to this
   path for the long haul?** Success in this endeavor
   requires commitment. You'll have to educate yourself about
   dog training and dog psychology, learn your legal rights

and responsibilities as a service dog handler, and be prepared to work through any problems that crop up (and they will).

If you notched five yesses, you're cleared to proceed! It is highly advisable, though not required, that you discuss your desire for a service dog with your therapist or medical provider.

Understanding Service Dog Interventions

Every service dog has official trained duties that make it a service dog, but that's only one part of the story. The other part is what a service dog brings to the table by virtue of its dogness and the bond between you, which is likely to be closer than with any other dog you've ever known. For people struggling with mental health issues, this second side is every bit as valuable as the first. Consider this: your therapist might not answer your distress call at 3 a.m. but your dog will, without question or judgement. Not just one time, but every night if you need it. When making the decision whether or not to take the PSD path, consider these "extras" too, which in practice are every bit as important as the official bits, even if that value isn't recognized legally.

Useful PSD Behaviors

Trained behaviors are what differentiate a PSD from an emotional support animal (ESA) or loving pet. The nature of the behaviors is specific to each individual handler's needs, so there's no fixed training program that's relevant to every service dog team. There are, however, things that are broadly useful in managing psychiatric disabilities. Techniques PSDs are frequently trained to employ include:

- Interruption (stop what you're doing)

- Distraction (get your mind on something else)

- Signaling (hey did you know...)

Hey, stop that!

In many situations interrupting is considered downright rude, but when a service dog does so, it's usually for a good reason. Interruption tasks are used to prevent unwanted behaviors or "snap you out of it," and may or may not be followed by a distraction task, which is an attempt to redirect your attention to better things, depending on the situation.

An SD will perform an interruption based on a trained cue, which is usually something they observe about the handler's behavior, which the handler may not even be aware of doing. The cue might be the handler staring into space, raising their voice, crying, or just about anything that you might want disrupted. The SD interrupts by nudging, pawing, or licking the handler until the handler responds. This is sometimes referred to as tactile stimulation, especially in the case of licking. Many people don't like getting their face licked by a dog, which means it can be especially useful in helping them break free from a dissociative spell or wake up from a nightmare.

Distraction tasks redirect the handler to a more desirable behavior. For example, a person who compulsively picks at their skin to the point of bleeding when nervous might have their dog trained to go get its grooming brush and present it to the handler whenever that occurs, or perhaps to nudge the handler's hands.

Excuse me, did you know...

Dogs are extremely observant of their surroundings, including their people. PSD handlers can take advantage of this by training their dog to notify them when a particular circumstance occurs. For example, many psychiatric medications can be very sedating, causing the patient to sleep through an alarm clock or smoke alarm or their baby crying, oblivious to the noise. In such cases the PSD can be trained to alert the handler by jumping up on the bed and nudging or licking the handler until they respond. A PSD can also be trained to remind the handler it's time to take their medication.

In addition to signaling their owner, PSDs can also be trained to signal someone else. For example, a PSD could be trained to notify a family member if the handler doesn't get up when an alarm clock goes off.

Bringing you back to the here and now

Grounding is a psychological technique that helps you break free from an intense emotional state by reorienting your focus to something in the present. It's used to help manage overwhelming feelings, anxiety, or dissociation, among other unpleasant sensations.

While the process of grounding is something you have to actively perform yourself, a service dog can serve as an aid and focal point to facilitate the process. One method is for the PSD to lick you on the face until you feel reoriented to the present. This is called tactile stimulation, and while some people find getting their face licked by a dog a little unpleasant, that's actually one reason why it's quite effective for something like bringing you out of a nightmare - because you can't ignore it for long! Another popular method used by handlers when sitting requires the dog to place its front paws and upper body across your lap. You then slowly run your hands through the dog's fur, concentrating on feeling the texture of each individual hair.

Smoothing rough moments

Deep pressure therapy (DPT) might sound like an exotic procedure you might undergo at an expensive new age spa, but it's actually a very common and exceedingly useful psychiatric service dog task you can get from your dog for free.

The purpose of DPT is to calm and soothe the handler and it can be quite effective. I once heard a handler remark that when her dog performs DPT, "It's like he's a giant Xanax." If you suffer from severe anxiety or panic attacks, you probably recognize Xanax as a rapid-acting anti-anxiety medication, so that's pretty high praise. A dog performs DPT by applying its body weight against the handler in particular ways, such as lying across the handler's chest and abdomen, effectively acting as an instant warm, weighted blanket.

Deep pressure touch like this helps the body relax and feel calm. There are many different techniques for applying DPT, and a PSD can be trained in multiple versions. Although some people argue this is simply cuddling with your dog, it becomes a task when your dog will perform it reliably on cue, in the manner you request, whether they feel like cuddling or not, and for as long as you need it.

Tasks like grounding, signaling, and DPT are really about empowering the handler by providing something constructive to do when unwelcome symptoms occur; rather than feel helpless and overwhelmed, the handler can take steps to improve the situation.

In addition to these common psychiatric tasks, PSDs can be trained to do work that provide help of a more physical nature. A person who takes medication that makes them dizzy when they stand up might have a large dog trained to brace itself and serve as an aide to balance if the handler suddenly gets dizzy. A PSD can fetch medicine, and if necessary a bottle of water to wash it down. Some PSDs do what's referred to as "light guide work," which can be leading a disoriented person back home or to an exit.

Working with Symptoms

Many PSD techniques can be successfully employed in a variety of situations. The following section provides a sampling of tasks often utilized to help with particular symptoms associated with psychiatric disabilities. Symptoms are presented in alphabetical order. Expect to adapt and expand on this list as you learn more about service dogs.

Anxiety & Panic

Although anxiety and panic disorders are technically different, these service dog interventions are helpful for either.

- Alert you to indications of rising anxiety/panic by pawing or nudging before you realize an attack is building. You can then take an action to prevent escalation or reduce the severity, such as leave the situation or take rescue meds.

- Provide a calming effect by applying DPT.

- Fetch emergency medications when you are too disabled by symptoms to get them.

- Summon a family member to come to your aid.

- Provide grounding assistance until the feelings abate.

Crowd Anxiety/Agoraphobia

Social anxiety and fear or hypervigilance when in public places is a common symptom of many psychiatric disorders. A PSD can provide crowd control as well as a sense of reassurance and protection. Having a PSD along makes it possible for some people who were previously too anxious to go out independently to do so; however, comfort provided by the mere presence of the SD does not count as work or a task under the ADA's legal definition of the term service dog, even though for people with acute anxiety, arguably it should. You can still benefit from it, but it won't count towards qualifying your dog as a legal SD. Things that a service dog can do that are considered tasks include:

- Use blocking techniques to maintain an area of space around you. The PSD is trained to place itself between you and other people, preventing them from approaching uncomfortably close. This can be accomplished in a variety of ways, depending on the size of the dog and the situation. A simple stand-stay between you and other people can work if the dog is reasonably large. Otherwise the dog may be trained to lie down lengthwise with its head near you and back end toward the person/people.

- Discourage people from coming up behind you. The PSD sits at your side, facing backwards (cover position) as if on guard.

- Provide grounding help to keep focus on the dog. This might include leaning into you, checking in by nudging you periodically, or other methods that draw your focus to the dog instead of their anxiety.

- Find a specific person or place if you become separated or overwhelmed in a crowd.

You might be surprised to learn that providing personal protection is not qualifying work or a task. Personal protection training (i.e. to bite or threaten on command) of service dogs is strongly discouraged.

Depression or Sadness

If you're feeling sad, isolated, or listless, a service dog can help simply by staying at your side and providing companionship. Although that doesn't count legally as a service dog task, it's invaluable nonetheless. There are some official things a PSD can do as well:

- Soothe you by applying DPT.

- Respond to crying or other signs of distress with distraction techniques such as licking or nudging.

Dissociation or Fear Paralysis

A PSD can be trained to recognize when its handler has frozen into a dissociated or paralyzed state and respond in ways that will "break the spell," such as:

- Interrupt the spell by nudging/licking/pawing you until you respond.

- Provide grounding assistance until the spell passes.

- Lead you to a safe place if you're disoriented, where you can remain until the spell passes.

Fear of Intruders

People who suffer from PTSD or some anxiety disorders may be afraid to enter a room for fear there's an intruder waiting inside. Even at home, a noise or simply waking up at night can send the heart rate soaring, and things get worse from there. The PSD can:

- Enter a room first and turn on the lights. A large PSD can flip a light switch. A smaller one can turn on a touch lamp.

- Search the premises to reassure you no one is there who shouldn't be. A PSD can be trained to check every room and bark if it discovers someone.

Hallucinations

A PSD can be helpful in providing a reality check for a person who is unsure whether another person or noise is actually present or a hallucination. It can indicate whether something is really there. Even a PSD not specifically trained in this task will provide evidence through its body language as to whether or not something concerning is really present. If the dog is lying relaxed beside you, chances are pretty high that nothing interesting is going on nearby. There are also ways to specifically train this. For example, PSD can be trained to approach and greet people on command. On seeing a person you are uncertain of, you would give a greet command, the PSD would move forward as directed, but finding no one to greet, return to you. In this way, you learn the person you think you see isn't really there.

Impaired Memory & Concentration

Both mental illnesses and the methods used to treat them can affect memory and attention. While a PSD can't bring these things back for you, there are things it can do to help fill in the gaps left behind, including:

- Find things like keys or telephone.

- Remind you to take medication or perform other daily routines.

- Help you regain focus through providing grounding assistance.

Medication Side Effects

Sleepiness, dizziness, hand tremors, and dry mouth are a few of the side effects that prescription medications can deliver alongside their beneficial effects. A service dog can make dealing with them a little easier. It can:

- Wake you up when an alarm clock isn't sufficient, when the doorbell rings, if the smoke alarm sounds, or other events occur that you might otherwise sleep through due to grogginess.

- Fetch a beverage to ease dry mouth. (Although this doesn't legally qualify as a task if you could easily do it yourself.)

- Pick things up off the floor so you can avoid bending over if that makes you dizzy.

- Provide balance support when going from sitting to standing if standing up makes your blood pressure drop.

Night Terrors/Nightmares

In addition to triggering immediate heart pounding, gut clenching distress, night terrors can result in sensations of fear and disorientation that persist even after waking up. Many times, if someone falls back to sleep without fully coming awake, the nightmare recurs, creating a vicious cycle that can make you dread falling asleep at night. Fortunately, there are several ways that a service dog can intervene in this process. It can:

- Wake you up from a nightmare by licking your face or nudging. Although some dogs do this naturally, many don't and it must be trained if you need it.

- Turn on lights to help dispel the nightmare and prevent you from falling back asleep too soon.

- Provide calming pressure (DPT).

- Provide grounding assistance to speed the resolution of post-nightmare disorientation.

Racing Thoughts

A service dog can help ease racing thoughts through tasks that provide distraction and soothing. It can:

- Distract you through tactile stimulation such as licking or by initiating a game.

- Provide calming through applying DPT.

Repetitive /Compulsive Behaviors

If you find yourself caught up rocking, twirling hair around your fingers, washing your hands long after they're clean and then doing it again, or engaged in other repetitive or compulsive behaviors, a PSD may be able to help you break free.

Interruption and redirection are the key tasks for this kind of symptom. The PSD will paw/nudge/lick you when you start displaying the behavior and can be trained to do something that will distract you from it and break the cycle, such as bring you a grooming brush so you can focus on grooming the dog instead.

Self-harm

Self-harm can take many forms, ranging from skin picking or pulling out hair, to scratching, burning, serious cutting and self-hitting. Dogs can be trained to respond to these types of behavior, but it's important to keep safety in mind when that response is shaped. For example, although it initially might seem like a good idea to train a dog to nudge the hand of a person who cuts to try to interrupt the process, in practice it's actually a terrible idea, as both the dog and the person might be injured in the process. A different response, such as providing DPT on request before the cutting starts, would be much better. For types of self-injury the handler is not aware of committing, or that don't create risk of injury to the dog, such as skin picking or hair pulling, interruption by nudging or pawing would be more appropriate.

- Interrupt behavior by pawing or nudging you. The PSD can also be trained to interrupt by barking, although that's not recommended if the task will be performed in public. You'll then ideally stop what you're doing and pay attention to your dog.

- Distract you by bringing a toy, leash, or brush and initiating play

- Notify family member in some cases, for example if you are cutting.

- Provide calming pressure (DPT) to de-escalate the situation that is leading you to feel like self-harming.

Sensory Overload

When sights, sounds, or sensations become overwhelming, there are several things a PSD can do to help turn things down a few notches.

- Apply calming pressure through DPT. This creates positive sensory input to help disrupt the impact of the overload.

- Provide grounding assistance to handler. This empowers the handler to turn their focus onto the grounding exercise and away from the troubling sensations.

Suicidal Ideation

Suicidal thoughts come in different varieties; some are immediate and severe and require getting professional help right away, while others may be more chronic thoughts that don't present an imminent danger but occupy your mind and mire you down. There are several ways a service dog can be trained to help with either kind.

- Provide distraction through tactile stimulation, such as licking, or by initiating an activity.

- Alert another person help is needed by fetching them or taking a note to them.

- Call 911 or other programmed number on special K9 phone.

Service Dogs are not Robots

As you've been reading about the impressive abilities of trained psychiatric service dogs, perhaps you've thought of dogs you've been fortunate enough to know. Most likely none of them were perfectly behaved all of the time! Service dogs, while dramatically better behaved than the average pet, are dogs first and medical assistance providers second. Even highly-trained PSDs aren't impeccably behaved all the time. They sometimes make mistakes or react in unexpected ways. If you're expecting perfection you will be disappointed and probably shouldn't get a service dog. Training, which is an ongoing process, will have its ups and downs, and you must be flexible and persistent to succeed.

As much as feasible, the PSD handler should personally take care of pretty much everything related to the dog, from feeding, to walking, to trips to the vet, especially when the partnership is new. This is key to building and strengthening the bond between dog and handler, which has extra importance with a PSD. Dogs need to go outside to potty multiple times a day and require regular exercise, the more the better. Don't expect to offload these duties to someone else. Others can pitch in, but the primary responsibility lies with the handler.

Service dogs for autism

Autism is often considered a neurological disorder rather than a psychological disorder, but like psychological disorders, it affects the way a person thinks and processes sensory information. Service dogs can help people with autism spectrum disorder (ASD) using many of the same behaviors that work for psychiatric conditions. For example, a service dog can be trained to interrupt stimming (repetitive self-stimulation) behaviors, which are common among people with ASD, and some of which are self-injurious. Grounding behaviors can help the handler break free of mental paralysis brought on by sensory overload. If the handler has speech difficulties, the dog can deliver a note to someone on their behalf. Many additional behaviors are possible, depending on the specific needs of the individual. In addition to performing work or tasks, a service dog can also serve as a social bridge, helping ease the social communication issues and resulting isolation that many people with ASD face.

There are many stories of autism service dogs creating life-altering changes for children and the family as a whole. This has led some parents to obtain a dog with the hope that it will bring about a similar change in their own child. However, the benefits occurred after pairing with a dog specifically trained to be an autism service dog, which is work that many dogs are simply not suited to do. A child who has meltdowns and difficulty controlling himself or herself physically can actually hurt a dog without meaning to, which is bad for the dog and can also result in the dog avoiding the child rather than bonding with him. The family ends up with a skittish dog who presents more needs than benefits. However, a dog specifically selected and trained with such behavior in mind can cope with it better. If you're considering an autism service dog for a child, your chances of success will be much better if you work with an organization that specializes in training service dogs for children with autism - from the beginning.

Although autism service dogs are most often associated with children, they can be a key to new independence for adults with ASD. Unfortunately, most service dog programs that train autism service dogs only provide them to children, so adults often have to owner train or work with a private trainer. The good news is that many adults with ASD successfully do so, finding new freedom and independence as a result.

Three-Way Service Dog Teams

In some cases, a person who would benefit greatly from a service dog isn't capable of fully managing the dog on their own. This most often occurs when the disabled person is a child, although it can be true for other people as well. The parent-child scenario is actually a pretty common situation, and in such cases a parent may act as a facilitator. The child (generally at least 10-12 years old) takes primary responsibility for care and safety of the service dog and is the recognized handler of the dog, but the parent supervises the process. The parent is responsible for ensuring that the dog's training program is adhered to, that health and safety concerns are met, and takes ultimate responsibility for the dog's well-being. The parent also supports and encourages the bonding process between the child and the service dog and helps the child cope with the ups and downs of becoming a service dog handler. The parent must remember that the key relationship is between the other two members of the team, and maintain a position as benevolent overseer.

Developing a Personal Task List

Figuring out what a service dog could do for you may be as easy as reading the examples in this chapter, or it might take a bit more work to pin down. As a starting point, make a list of your most debilitating symptoms related to your disability (or disabilities), including any medication side effects. You might wish to invite your medical providers, close friends, or family members to contribute items to the list. There may be things that are apparent to others but no so obvious to you. You may generate additional ideas by reading the official diagnostic description of your disorder(s) and its associated characteristics in the current Diagnostic and Statistical Manual of Mental Disorders (DSM). Remember that a service dog can be cross-trained to respond to multiple disabilities, so if you have any physical disabilities, consider those as well.

Once you have your symptom list, start thinking about how each item might be mitigated. Do you currently rely on a "human service person" to help you navigate daily living? What does that person do for you that a dog could do? Spend some time surfing the web for ideas. There are quite a few blogs published by PSD handlers, and you may run across a novel solution to a problem you also have.

"Task shopping" is discouraged, however. Task shopping means looking for tasks you don't really need in order to qualify your dog as a service dog. Conducting thorough research to uncover tasks that would potentially help *you* is simply being smart! How are you supposed to know what's possible unless you dig?

Once you have your initial list, revisit each item and assess how reasonable it is. Some of the items might be easy to teach, others could take many months, and a few might not be possible. For example, "make me happy" is not something you can train a dog to do, although having a dog might improve your overall mood. This can be a good time to talk to a professional dog trainer about your list - is it realistic? How long would it take to train these things? Review the list with close family members or friends - do they have anything they would add or remove?

Resolving the work/task debate

The ADA defines a service dog as any dog that is individually trained to "do work or perform task(s)" that benefit an individual with a disability. Those four, harmless-looking words have led to a great deal of stress, strain, and debate within the service dog community. They have triggered many heated discussions that start with: "My dog does X, is that a task or work?" and continue with rounds of arguments on both sides. It's a distinction that's not actually worth getting hot and bothered over because the answer doesn't matter! If your dog performs a trained behavior that mitigates your disability, it counts, regardless of how someone classifies it.

Although technically work and tasks are different things, the definitions do overlap to the extent that a particular behavior can't always be pinned firmly into one category or the other. If you want to categorize your dog's behaviors anyway, here are some criteria you can use:

- **Task** - Most analogous to a specific assignment. For example: Pick up that item. Give me DPT.

- **Work** - An open-ended thing the dog is "on call" to do as needed, without it being specifically requested. For example, a PSD may be trained to observe if their handler starts showing a particular sign of stress, such as clenched fists, and respond by pawing the handler's leg. The dog might need to do this anytime, anywhere and is not specifically requested to do so.

These definitions do overlap, as a behavior might be requested specifically at times and be delivered as the result of something the dog has observed at other times. Lest you have any continued concern that a service dog must be "task-trained," here's a quote from an explanation of ADA regulations published by the federal government in 2010:

> *"The Department received a number of comments in response to the NPRM proposal urging the removal of the term "do work" from the definition of a service animal. These commenters argued that the Department should emphasize the performance of tasks instead. The Department disagrees. Although the common definition*

> *of work includes the performance of tasks, the definition of work is somewhat broader, encompassing activities that do not appear to involve physical action."*
>
> Furthermore, contrary to a prevalent myth, the minimum number of tasks (or work) your dog needs to do to meet the legal definition of service dog is one. So if you read somewhere that a dog must be trained in multiple tasks to qualify as a service dog, you'll know that's wrong: tasks aren't the only thing that qualifies and one is enough (though most dogs do more)! More importantly, don't get caught up worrying about whether the behavior your dog performs is a work or a task; as long as it's a trained behavior that mitigates your disability, that's what matters.

Considering Social Implications

If you get a service dog, your family, social life, and employment options will be impacted. You might expect the changes to all be positive as the service dog brings you increased independence and a new ability to navigate life. There are, however, potential trade-offs to consider. They may be well worth making in exchange for the changes a PSD can bring to your life, but it really depends on your personal situation.

Factoring in Friends and Family

The people in your life will be affected by the addition of a service dog to your household, and it's only fair to consider the impact on those around you. There will be expenses, inconveniences, and dog hair, and that's just the easy stuff. There can be a surprising amount of resistance from family members and friends due to their own concerns, some of which might be quite reasonable. Other people have feelings, needs, and insecurities also. It's important to address these issues up front, before any ugly surprises derail your efforts or unexpectedly damage key relationships. You may decide it's worth getting a service dog anyway, or perhaps decide it's not such a great idea at this particular point in your life. Here are some questions to ask:

- How will your family members or "significant other" feel about your disability becoming publicly visible? Having a service dog at your side publicly labels you as a person with a disability. If your disability has previously been "invisible" and/or private information, this can be a big deal as it won't be "invisible" any more.

- Will your friends and family accept your service dog accompanying you on outings? This draws attention to them as well as to you. It also adds potential inconveniences.

- How will they feel about your bringing your service dog with you to their home when you visit?

- Does anyone in your household suffer from pet allergies?

- Are there children in the household who will want to interact with the dog?

- Are there other pets in the household? Although this certainly isn't a disqualifying factor, it's important to realize that there will be different expectations for the service dog versus a family pet, and you and other household members must be prepared to treat them differently.

While you might be willing to sacrifice a friend or two for the sake of improving your daily life, spouses and other family members are another matter. While you can probably work around concerns of a relative who doesn't live with you, the support of other people in your household can make or break your chances for success.

Some people insist that a spouse or significant other must be totally onboard with going everywhere as a threesome (you, partner, SD) or the idea is a nonstarter, but that's not automatically the case. If your partner thinks it's a great idea for you to have a PSD but at the same time feels (perhaps acutely) uncomfortable in the spotlight of attention that a service dog brings and doesn't want to go out as a threesome, you have an option: when you're out together, leave your SD home (after all, you'll have the support of your partner), otherwise take your SD with you. Your partner's well-being matters as much as yours; be accepting of each other's needs and compromise in the way that helps you both the most.

These aren't always easy talks to have or decisions to make, but you should indeed address them before making a decision about a service dog. Just trusting that things will sort themselves out might be easier but you'll be setting yourself up for trouble down the road.

Employment Matters

Having a service dog can affect your employment options. A PSD can be a critical aid that enables you to enter or return to the workforce when your disability previously made it impossible. This is more feasible for some types of employment than others. Desk jobs are the easiest because the SD can remain unobtrusively at your feet most of the time.

While there are laws regarding employers making "reasonable accommodations" and allowing you to bring your service dog to work, you may have to fight for this right and prove your need for such an accommodation. Some employers will happily allow it, but others not so much. The Job Accommodation Network (**http://askjan.org**) provides authoritative and accurate information about workplace accommodations and the ADA. If their website doesn't have the answers you need, you can call them with specific questions.

A service dog will perform work and tasks for you and provide companionship, big pluses for everyone, but it will also affect your life in other ways that are not so beneficial and can even cause problems that may outweigh the benefits - only you can decide based on your particular situation.

Managing Public Encounters

Being accompanied by a service dog will bring you attention wherever you go. Many people will just look and politely go about their business, but others will ask you questions: What kind of dog is that? Who are you training it for? Why do you need a service dog? You don't look disabled.

You can count on questions like this nearly every time you go through a checkout line and it will happen in other places too. For some PSD handlers this is no big deal, and they seize such moments as opportunities to educate the public about service dogs. Extroverts may even find this a benefit, as dog-talk provides an easy conversation starter. For people with acute self-consciousness or public anxiety, however, this can be intolerable. Chapter 9: Social Skills for Dogs and Handlers offers strategies for minimizing such encounters or making them less triggering, but they cannot be completely avoided.

It's also possible you will encounter access challenges. An access challenge occurs when you enter an establishment with your SD and an employee or other official tells you that you cannot bring your dog in, even though legally you can. Then you must either persuade them they are wrong (at the time or through management after the fact) or leave. Thankfully such confrontations are infrequent, but from time to time they do happen.

You can get around a lot of these potential problems by making your service dog at-home-only and not taking it with you when you go places. While this is definitely not ideal, it's an option. People who can't tolerate the scrutiny that comes with public access can still obtain substantial benefits by utilizing a PSD at home, and that team will still have all the rights and protections accorded under the ADA.

There is no doubt that the logistics, inconveniences, explanations, and care obligations of service dog ownership can be overwhelming to some people already struggling with psychiatric issues. Many others, however, find that these responsibilities actually add motivation and structure to daily living. PSDs provide disability-mitigating tasks, companionship, and unconditional love, a unique, transformative package with the power to change lives. They cannot cure what ails you, but they can make coping with it a lot easier.

Chapter 4

Obtaining a Service Dog from a Program

In This Chapter

➢ Selecting a service dog provider

➢ Working through the application process

➢ Applying to programs

Service dog programs are the first place many people turn to in the hunt for an able canine assistant. The idea of a ready-to-go service dog is very appealing, and program dogs, as they're called, have a lot of positives: they're pre-selected for temperament and health, past puppyhood, already trained in obedience, public access skills, and individualized tasks specific to your needs. Most programs provide ongoing support and will help troubleshoot any problems that arise. What's not to like?

There are actually some pretty good reasons not to go the program route, with lack of availability and expense topping the list. If you're a military veteran with service-related PTSD, you have a decent chance of finding a program that will equip you with a PSD at little or no charge; otherwise, get ready for a long, expensive, uphill climb.

Programs that offer trained psychiatric service dogs to the general public are exceedingly rare. They typically carry a $10,000-

$20,000 price tag, a multi-year waiting period, and come with a bunch of strings attached. Service dogs for psychiatric needs are still a relatively new concept, and there just aren't a lot of programs producing them yet. The process of producing a trained service dog is time consuming, expensive, and not guaranteed as a dog can wash out anywhere along the way for a variety of reasons. So the supply is limited. A substantial percentage of that, often funded by donations, is earmarked for military veterans with service-connected disabilities. That's the current reality of PSD supply and demand. It's possible to obtain a service dog from a program and live happily ever after, but it's not going to be easy.

If you're considering going the program route, don't make the mistake of thinking that getting a program dog is going to spare you from doing any work! You will still have to maintain the dog's training for the rest of its time in service, just as you would if you trained it yourself. You may be required to travel to the organization's facility annually for a "tune-up" session or "re-certification" to make certain that you keep up the dog's skills, but even without that, you will need to become knowledgeable in dog training and dog psychology and practice!

The alternative to program dogs is to obtain and train a dog yourself. That's no walk in the park either, but many people are quite able to train a PSD, either on their own or with the help of a professional trainer. Intimate involvement throughout the training process allows the dog to become more attuned to you and your baseline emotional state, which is one of the reasons a lot of people in the PSD community recommend owner-training. Table 4.1 lists major pros and cons of going the program route.

Table 4-1: Weighing the Benefits of Obtaining a Service Dog from a Program

Pros	*Cons*
Dog arrives fully trained and ready to work. No risk of dog washing out.	Can be difficult or impossible to find a program that will accept you.

Avoids questions of legitimacy that sometimes accompany owner-trained dogs as your dog seems more "official."	Cost is often prohibitive.
Comes with ongoing support relationship with provider organization.	No say in breed of dog. You receive whatever they give.
Fundraising can be easier, especially if the dog is coming from a nonprofit program as donations would be to a charitable organization instead of directly to you and are tax-deductible.	You may not legally own the dog and may have to return it under certain circumstances.
	Usually a one- to two-year wait or longer.
	May incur ongoing obligations to the program such as required additional visits.

Some people realistically aren't able to undertake owner training or have other reasons for opting for a program-provided service dog. If a program dog would best meet your needs, then break out the file folders and notebooks (electronic or paper) and start taking notes about how the process usually works and things to watch out for. This dog, and likely the agency it came from, will be in your life 10 years or more! It's important to do everything possible to ensure a good match. The service dog industry is completely unregulated, so it's up to you to be an informed consumer.

You'll need to do a bit of research to find specific service dog programs that mesh with your needs. For example, some service dog programs work with rescue dogs, others breed and raise their own candidates. A program may serve a specific geographic area or a particular population, such as veterans with combat-related disabilities. Some programs will foot some or all of the cost of the process while others will charge you $10,000 or more and expect payment up front.

Finding and Evaluating Service Dog Programs

It's important to be careful and thorough in selecting and applying to programs. There are good and bad programs - even some fraudulent programs - and when you're eager to have a service dog at your side sooner rather than later, it's easy to overlook red flags and rush toward the prize, only to find that instead of the life-saving service dog you expected, you've got a problem. Be methodical, do your homework, and you'll maximize your chances for success.

Getting Organized

If you haven't started an organizational system for your service dog search yet, now is the time. You can do it with pen and paper, but taking the time to set up a spreadsheet or word processing document will pay great dividends; you'll be able to store links to program web sites and gain the ability to easily sort and search. Your recordkeeping system should include program contact information, cost, if you've contacted them yet, and the status of your application. Include any distinguishing information that's important to you. Try to organize this so you can tell at a glance which programs you have or haven't applied to and what your next step will be.

Create an initial list of criteria that are important to you: Do you need a dog that is strictly a PSD or one that also provides additional functions such as mobility assistance or allergen detection? How far are you willing and able to travel for this? Can you pay full price for a dog or are programs that offer free or low cost placements your only option?

Nonprofit vs for-profit providers

Many service dog programs are operated as nonprofit organizations, but others are run as for-profit businesses. This can be a point of confusion, leading people to wonder if one is better than the other. Actually, neither is automatically superior, they simply reflect different organizational structures. People often believe that nonprofits get their name because they don't make a profit from their activities, which is a myth. Like other business, nonprofits strive to generate revenues that exceed expenses - otherwise they would not be able to continue operating for long! Nor are all for-profit businesses in it strictly for the money; many are dedicated toward serving the social good. So what are the differences? Table 4.2 highlights the major distinctions.

Table 4-2: Comparing Nonprofit and For-Profit Entities

Nonprofit Organization	*For-Profit Business*
Exists to serve a primary purpose other than making a profit, such as furthering a social cause or advocating for a particular point of view	Exists to earn a profit. May also have a mission of providing public benefit.
Public organizations, owned by the public, not the person(s) who started it.	Owned by individuals or shareholders
Money to operate comes from donations, grants, and revenue	Money to operate comes from owner investments/financing and revenue
Profits are reinvested into ongoing operations	Profits may be reinvested or distributed to owners/shareholders
Often exempt from paying federal taxes and some state/local taxes	Pays taxes
Money donated to organization is deductible from donor's personal income tax if organization has tax-exempt status	Money invested by owners/shareholders or donated is not deductible from personal taxes

Each organizational form has advantages and drawbacks. Whether a service dog provider is nonprofit or for-profit will likely affect how much you will have to pay. It also can be easier to solicit fundraising donations for a nonprofit. Otherwise, neither is automatically better than the other.

Finding Service Dog Providers

Once you have your criteria, it's time to hit the Internet and begin your search. The website for Assistance Dogs International (ADI), which can be accessed at **www.assistancedogsinternational.org**, is a good place to start. ADI is a membership organization for nonprofit assistance dog organizations. It operates an accreditation system and maintains a searchable directory of programs. Although this is a good place to start, this directory is far from comprehensive as only members of ADI are included. A program's inclusion in the directory provides some indication of its legitimacy, but it's not a guarantee. You'll still need to perform your own research to confirm its current status. Another list can be found at **dogcapes.com/trainers.html**.

Google is your friend here, but also your enemy, as it will offer up programs indiscriminately. It will not discern legitimate, relevant programs you might qualify for from others that are inappropriate, out of date, unproven, or of poor quality. It's up to you to separate the wheat from the chaff. Good search phrases to try include "psychiatric service dog" or "PTSD dog" or "service dog application" or "service dog organizations."

If possible, network with other experienced service dog owners. If you don't know any personally, you can connect with some online through Facebook groups or service dog sites such as **ServiceDogCentral.org** and **PsychDogPartners.org**. Chapter 8: Getting to Know the Service Dog Community guides you to helpful resources.

Assessing a Service Dog Organization

While inclusion in the Assistance Dogs International (ADI) directory is a positive sign, don't rely on that as your only criteria for determining if a program is legit. Before you even contact the organization directly, there are some things you can check:

- ✓ **Do a BBB check.** Check with the Better Business Bureau where the program is located to see if there are any unresolved complaints against the program.

✓ **If organization is a nonprofit, review its financial reports and structure online.** Nonprofit charities must file IRS form 990 each year, which summarizes revenues and expenses. Sites such as CharityNavigator.org and GuideStar.org collect and collate information about the current status of nonprofit charities and are free to use. Make sure the information on these sites matches what you've been told.

✓ **Join the Facebook Group: Service Dog Organizations & Trainer Reviews.** This is a small group but it contains detailed reviews from people who have actually received a dog from particular service dog organizations.

✓ **Google "organization-name scam" and see if anything pops up.** Just in case.

If the organization passes muster, go ahead and contact them and start asking your questions directly. Before you sign on any dotted lines, ask for a list of previous clients you can contact as references and talk to some of them. There are many good service dog organizations out there, but there are also plenty of scammers, and there are also trainers who think that, by virtue of experience training dogs, they have what it takes to be a service dog trainer but then find out they are in over their heads and things fall apart. To be safe, be a skeptic. Watch out for these red flags in particular:

- Places young dogs or puppies as full service dogs. Full service dogs are generally at least 18 months old.

- If a 501(c)(3) nonprofit, resists giving you their financial information.

- There is no formal application process.

- Doesn't want you to visit their facility. You should be able to visit the kennel, meet the trainer(s) and dogs.

- Doesn't want you to have your attorney review their contract.

- No working teams you can meet. You should be able to meet and interact with previous clients.

- Doesn't ask you lots of personal questions about yourself and what you need in a service dog. They just want your credit card and you can have a dog.

- Want all the money up front. A portion up front is reasonable, but requiring it all in advance is suspicious. Once they have your money, they have less incentive to move forward.

- They claim a 100% success rate in placing service dogs. Even the most carefully selected dogs can wash out, and some handler/dog matches just don't work. Failure is part of this process and should be planned for.

- No plan exists for continuing support after placement. Training is ongoing and should be provided for in some way.

If possible, visit the facility and observe the dogs in training. Above all, resist the temptation to rush this process. It's natural to want move as quickly as possible toward the exciting goal of having a fully trained service dog at your side, but take care to do so in a deliberate, wise manner.

Understanding the Application Process

Before you start the hunt for a specific service dog program, preview how the process of applying for and receiving a service dog typically works. Every program is a little unique in this respect, but there are more similarities than differences. Figure 4-1 summarizes the typical process, which is also described in detail below.

Figure 4-1: The Service Dog Application Process

Submit pre-screening application

Submit full application + application fee

Complete personal interview

Sign contract + pay "commmitment fee"

Get matched with a dog in training

Attend team training & bring dog home

Complete follow-up training & commitments

Although the specifics will vary among organizations, the process of applying for a service dog typically goes something like this:

1) **Submit a pre-screening application.** This is a basic screening tool used to assess your interest and the match between your needs and the program's services. For example, if the program only serves people within a 300-mile radius of its facilities you're three states over, or you need a dog to also help with mobility and they don't train for that, you won't go past this step. Usually there isn't a charge for this, and frankly, since you're submitting an application to be allowed to submit an application, I would be suspicious of any program that asked for one. A pre-application might be accepted through the organization's website, via email, regular mail, or fax. You should know if you'll pass this by reading the organization's materials closely and understanding who they serve. If the information you need isn't on the organization's website, it's okay to call them and ask. Passing this does NOT mean they agree to give you a dog, only that they are willing to

move to the next step. If your pre-application is approved, you move on to step two. Some programs skip this step and go straight to the application (and the fee).

2) **Submit a full application with application fee.** This will be longer and more detailed. You will need to provide detailed descriptions of your disabilities, limitations, and expectations regarding a service dog. You will also likely be required to submit a letter from a doctor documenting your condition in detail (you'll have to sign a medical release form). Personal references may be required, and those references will be asked personal questions about you (What kind of person is Mr. X?). Applications will often ask about your living situation to ensure it's suitable for a dog and that you have the wherewithal to physically and financially care for one. You will be asked who lives with you, if you have other pets (for some programs this will exclude you), and if you have any previous experience with dogs. You may be asked if you have a criminal record. There is also likely to be a "financial worksheet" of some kind included in the package, with questions about your income and if/where you work. You will need to provide evidence that you can pay for the dog. Some programs will help you with fundraising and/or provide scholarships, but the degree of help varies considerably, and when it comes down to it, the money has to add up for the dog to be placed with you. There are programs that provide financial assistance for some of the cost, but not many are available to ordinary people seeking a service dog to help with psychiatric disabilities.

This lengthy application is usually available via the program's website or sent via email for you to print out, complete, and submit via mail along with the application fee. Keep a copy of all forms for your records. It's a good idea to send it via Certified Mail or at least get Delivery Confirmation service.

It's important that you are completely honest when filling out these applications. As invasive as some questions may seem, the agency needs to get a very complete picture of your situation to determine how a dog might be trained to help you and to choose an appropriate dog to pair with you. In addition, you will most likely need to sign an affirmation that everything is true and that the dog can be reclaimed if you've fibbed in any way. Best not to risk going there...

Your application should be considered within a reasonable amount of time - many organizations cite 30 days as the response window. If you get the green light for the next step, you're well on your way.

3) **Complete a personal interview.** They've already met you on paper, now they get to meet you in person. The interview may be conducted at the organization's office, in your home, or in some cases over the phone or via video. If you were thorough in completing the paperwork up to this point, there should be no big surprises here. After all, you're used to answering all those incredibly personal questions by now. Some programs make a home visit, or if you're far away, request a video showing what your home and yard look like. This is also an opportunity for you to interview the program as well. Clear up any lingering questions you might have about what happens when and who is responsible for what.

4) **Sign contracts, pay a "commitment fee," and get placed on a waiting list for a dog.** The organization should go over the contracts with you in detail. Be sure anything you sign matches what you understand, particularly where it comes to ongoing obligations between you and the organization. Double check your application "must know" question list to be certain everything mentioned in the next section, "Questions You Must Ask," is covered. The program should give you an estimate of how long you'll be on the waiting list, typically one to two years or the wait may be linked to your fundraising progress. When you pay the remaining balance varies by program; it might be before you can get matched, before you take delivery of the dog, or at another point.

5) **Get matched with a dog!** This does not mean your dog is ready to come home with you yet, but it's a major step in

that direction. It means a particular dog, which has been assessed as likely to meet your needs, has been pegged with your name. It's likely that the dog won't have completed its training at this point, but you may receive pictures and progress reports. The dog will receive further individualized training based on your needs.

6) **Attend team training, bring service dog home.** You will travel to the organization's facility (in some cases they will come to you but most often the handler goes to the facility) and meet your new service dog. For the next one to two weeks, you will get to know your dog and work under the supervision of the facility's trainers. There may be other handlers going through the same process in a group situation. You may stay at the facility or at a nearby hotel. You will learn how to control and command your dog and how to care for its needs. Most likely your training will involve field trips to places where you can practice your public access skills. You will receive education regarding the legal rights and responsibilities of service dog ownership. Near the end of this training "boot camp" you will probably be given a test to assess your performance as a service dog team. Then you get to bring your dog home and truly begin your journey as a team.

7) **Complete follow-up training and commitments as required by the program.** A program may require periodic "recertification" of your dog's training or provide for follow-up training and consultations.

Questions You Must Ask

Receiving a service dog from a program isn't simply a matter of exchanging cash for a trained service dog. Often there are substantial strings attached. You may be surprised to learn that it's not uncommon for the organization to retain legal ownership of the dog either for the first year or permanently, and that they can exercise a right to reclaim the dog if you violate any terms of your agreement with them, or if other specified conditions occur. You may be required to allow the organization to use your photo and story for promotional purposes. The quantity and thickness of the strings attached to your dog will vary greatly depending on the organization. Most likely they will all be spelled out for you quite clearly by the time you're asked to sign on the bottom line, but it's best to know closer to the beginning of the process. If the information isn't offered, you need to ask at least these questions:

- ✓ What breeds of dogs do you use and where do you get them? (How are they selected for temperament and health?)

- ✓ How many service dogs have you placed?

- ✓ What training methods do you use?

- ✓ How long after my application is accepted will I receive a dog?

- ✓ Who owns the dog you place with me?

- ✓ Is my payment considered purchasing the dog or a donation to the organization?

- ✓ Am I required to use/display the training program's vest/harness/patch or other identifying items or can I use any that I prefer?

- ✓ Are there any conditions under which you would repossess the dog from me?

- ✓ What is the arrangement for follow-up support and help resolving any problems that might arise?

- ✓ Are there ongoing requirements/financial commitments such as annual recertification through the program?

- ✓ If required to return annually for a "training check-up/tune-up," what happens if I happen to move across the country or even out of the country?

- ✓ When the dog retires from service, do I get to keep the dog as my pet?

✓ If the dog dies or is unable to perform as a service dog for any reason, will you refund my money?

As you begin digging into the details of specific service dog program applications, you may find a few more to add to the list.

Questions You Must Answer

The service dog organization is going to want to get to know you very well. Just like you, they want the best chance for a successful service dog partnership. To that end, you can expect to answer a very long list of questions about your medical condition and your personal life. It might feel intrusive, but that's how this works. It's a necessary part of pairing the right dog, with the proper training, to a compatible handler. Here's a sampling of things you can expect to be asked:

✓ How old are you? What are your height and weight?

✓ What is the nature of your disability(ies)?

✓ When did it start?

✓ How does that impact your life on a daily basis?

✓ Do you use any assistive devices, such as a brace, crutches, or a "grabber" to reach things?

✓ Do you have other pets? What kinds/ages/temperaments?

✓ Do you consider yourself a "dog" person?

✓ Who are the other members of the household and how do they feel about you getting a service dog?

✓ Are there children? How old?

✓ What is your employment situation?

✓ What do you expect from a service dog?

✓ Are you able to help in fundraising for your dog?

✓ Do you have a fenced yard?

✓ Can you afford $900-$1200 a year for food, vet bills, and supplies?

✓ Who will care for the dog if you are unable to?

✓ Can you travel to our facility for two weeks of graduation training?

✓ How will you pay for this?

Questions like these will appear on the application form and reappear during the personal interview.

Submitting Applications

Each time you have contact with a program, update your tracking system to reflect the date of contact and current status of your interaction with that program. Dates and details have a way of slipping away if not recorded.

Many people wonder if they should apply to one program at a time or go ahead and apply to several simultaneously. There is no hard and fast rule dictating this, but you'll likely have to pay an application fee to each program, which for many people is the deciding factor. Also, if you have a clear preference for a particular program, it's best to apply to that one and wait for the results before moving on. Otherwise, consider applying to multiple programs, see who accepts your application and what terms, including length of wait, they propose. There's no need to share with anyone that you're taking a multi-pronged approach; chances are that you won't be accepted by every program you apply to any way. You may not be a match for their program, there may not be dogs available, the program may be on hiatus - there are many different reasons a program may not move forward.

Most programs will specify how long you can expect to wait before receiving a determination from them as to whether you will move forward to the next step. Note these dates in your files and be sure to follow up if that date comes and goes with no word. Don't let your application linger in extended limbo.

As mentioned above, getting accepted into a program is only the first step; you still need to be matched with a dog, the dog will receive further individualized training, and then you'll be trained to work with your new partner. The service dog organization should keep you updated throughout this process. It can be a long wait - up to several years in some cases - but if you're lucky it can be shorter. Stick with it and you'll get there.

Chapter 5

Deciding to Owner-Train

In This Chapter

- ➤ A look at the path to a fully trained service dog
- ➤ Assessing your readiness to make the journey
- ➤ Where to find your service dog prospect
- ➤ Characteristics to look for in your future service dog
- ➤ Mapping out a training plan
- ➤ Tools to keep you on track
- ➤ Graduating from in-training to in-service

Many people choose to train their own psychiatric service dog rather than acquire one from a service dog program. For many it's a matter of necessity - they don't qualify for any programs, can't afford those that might approve their application, or there simply aren't any programs that are accessible to them. Others feel owner-training is the superior route. They prefer to be in control from start to finish, and especially don't like the idea that someone else might retain legal ownership of their service dog, which some programs do.

Being deeply involved in your dog's training is beneficial to both sides of the team. The continuous close contact of owner-training facilitates the dog learning what your "normal" is, and subsequently recognizing signals that you're leaving normal behind and need an intervention. From your end of the leash, the process of training your PSD helps you become more aware and intimately knowledgeable of your mental health. You must understand your triggers and symptoms in order to train the dog. Because of the intensive work of training, your connection with your SD will be very close. Table 5-1 summarizes the major pros and cons of owner training.

Table 5-1: Weighing the Benefits of Owner-training a Service Dog

Pros	*Cons*
No waiting list	Requires a great deal of time and commitment to complete training
Greater choice in breed and size of dog	Riskier - Risk of washout assumed by handler instead of program
Opportunity to build bond with dog from earliest stages and for dog to learn handler's emotional states	Can feel less "official" than a program dog even though equal under federal laws
Cost is more spread out than when getting a program dog	Some people have difficulty training their own SD due to their disability. For example, severe depression or social anxiety can impede progress

Previewing the Journey

The path from average canine to service dog is pretty straightforward, and can be summed up in five steps:

1) **Obtain a prospect.** Prospect and candidate are interchangeable terms meaning a dog that has potential to become your service dog, based on temperament and initial screening criteria you have defined based on your wants and needs. This crucial step is discussed in detail later in this chapter.

2) **Learn basic obedience and socialization.** During this time your dog should master commands such as sit, stay, lie down, come when called, walking on a loose leash, and of course be housebroken. Although not formally required, many handlers use the American Kennel Association (AKC) Canine Good Citizen (CGC) test as a target for confirming initial obedience training. During this time your SD should also work on socialization skills, gaining exposure to many different people and other dogs.

3) **Start training public access skills.** A service dog must behave in a reliable and mannerly ways in public settings such as restaurants, grocery stores, on public transportation, and in other venues. For example, they should not scarf up food left on the floor, sniff products on shelves, or become excited or unruly while working. A public access test (PAT) may be used to assess a dog's readiness for working in public by evaluating their level of public access skills.

4) **Start task/work training.** You can start training disability-mitigating tasks pretty much at any point. It isn't necessary to complete public access training before beginning this step. You'll need to proof task training in public venues eventually.

5) **Graduate to full SD status.** At this point the dog should be able to pass a public access test (PAT) and perform at least one disability-mitigating task reliably. Although passing a PAT isn't a legal requirement, it's a good idea.

This initial training period lasts from six months to two years, depending on the dog you start with and your commitment. In general:

- **Puppy:** Eighteen months to two years. Although a dog may learn faster and be able to do work for you before then, most dogs are not mentally mature with a stable temperament until about two to three years old.

- **Adult dog with ideal temperament and no behavior problems:** six months to one year.

- **Adult dog with some issues:** 12 -18 months.

Throughout this time, expect to spend an average of 20 -30 minutes per day on training, plus additional time for exercise, grooming, and other care. Puppies require more time, as does resolving problem behaviors. Within this time, it's normal to encounter periods of rapid learning followed by periods of regression when your service dog in training (SDiT) stops performing skills that seemed solid.

It's not just the dog who will encounter pauses and regressions, most owner-trainers do as well. Life intervenes, people become overwhelmed by something or too depressed to get out of bed for a few days or otherwise held back by their disability. As long as you keep steady forward progress, a little down time here and there is no big deal.

Before you Begin

Owner training can be a rewarding choice that brings partnership with a PSD into the realm of possibility for people who otherwise wouldn't be able to obtain a service dog, but it's not right for everyone. Before deciding to owner-train, take the time to develop a complete understanding of what you're getting into and to assess whether it's a realistic option for you. Owner-training does not mean going it 100% alone; most owner trainers seek assistance from a professional dog trainer, either on a regular basis starting with puppy selection or as needed to help meet particular training goals.

Whether you picture yourself teaming up with a trainer or following a do-it-yourself route with the help of books, videos, and the internet, there are several things to carefully consider before you begin.

✓ Be certain you understand the facts about owner training and your own suitability to undertake it.

✓ Consider your "dogability" level. What do you know about dogs and how experienced are you in handling them?

✓ Think about what you will do if the dog washes out.

Recognizing Owner Training Myths

Owner training is the most accessible route for many people seeking a psychiatric service dog, but don't make the mistake of assuming it's faster, drastically cheaper, or a slam-dunk undertaking. Here's why these common myths aren't true:

1) **It's not faster** - There's no wait list to get started, but you'll still have to wait quite a while before you have a working service dog at your side. You'll wait to find the right dog, wait through fear stages, wait through teenage back-sliding, correcting any behavioral issues, and more. If you start with an adult dog with a perfect temperament and basic obedience training in place, you could potentially reach full steam in six months, but for most one and a half to two years is more realistic.

2) **It's not necessarily cheaper** - You may have less cash outlay up front, but you will most likely be paying for professional training assistance (recommended for everyone). The first two years or so of a program dog's food and medical bills have been paid by the program. You will be paying these yourself. So it may or may not be cheaper, although the costs will be more spread out.

3) **Not everyone can do it** - Training your own SD isn't just about time and money, it also requires great dollops of patience, commitment, persistence, and perseverance. You will need training as much as your dog does, because a large part of successful dog training is training the owner how to behave and respond in various situations. You must be ready to open yourself to the firehose of knowledge that's about to come your way and drink it in. Some people are unable to become successful dog trainers, no matter how hard they try, just like some people will never become competent carpenters or complete a gymnastic tumbling run.

Are You Dog Ready?

If you have no experience with dogs, get some before you consider undertaking training your own service dog. No amount of reading, discussion, web surfing, or forum participation is going to prepare you adequately if you've never lived with one before. As a starting point, consider auditing an obedience class to observe how different dogs and handlers interact. You may be able to do this through a local "big box" store like PetCo or through a local dog training club. Consider volunteering for a local no-kill shelter, helping to exercise and care for the animals. Fostering is another option. A dog you foster lives in your home temporarily, until it is adopted. You'll be taking care of it 24/7 and can even work on improving basic obedience and manners, making it more adoptable. Many animal shelters and rescue groups operate fostering programs. To find rescue groups close by, use **PetFinder.com** to search for dogs in your zip code, and the results will include the names of sponsoring rescue organizations.

Successful owner-trainers tend to have a background that includes previous dog training experience, the more the better. If you don't, then your owner training plan (and budget) needs to closely involve someone who does, from the very beginning.

This is an undertaking that requires commitment for success. Expect to practice daily whatever you're currently working during the training period. You can miss a day here or there but not a week or two. You must be willing to take your dog out in public with you and endure potential stressful encounters if people question you about the dog.

Many states have laws that require businesses to give access to service dogs in training as well as full service dogs, but some do not or only recognize certain types of service dogs in training or those trained by "professional" trainers. In states that don't grant access to owner trainers, public access training must be conducted in pet-friendly places only or places where you have gained explicit permission.

Public access training is where many owner trainers run into a wall or fall short. They do great on teaching tasks, but the public work isn't given the attention it needs. It's possible to find people to help you with this, so make sure you do so if necessary.

What is Your Washout Plan?

If you decide to owner train, you will be investing huge amounts of time, energy, money, and love into your service dog candidate, along with a whole lot of hope. It's an unfortunate reality of service dog training that even the most carefully selected dog may turn out to be unsuitable for work as a service dog. Taking a dog out of service dog training is referred to as "washing" the dog. It's a difficult and often heart-breaking decision to make, but it happens to owner trainers fairly often. If you elect to owner train, you must be prepared for the possibility that you will have to wash your dog. If that happens, what will you do? Will you be able to get another service dog candidate and keep your existing dog as a pet or would you re-home the washed dog? Could you bear to do that?

Any of the following reasons can lead to a service dog candidate needing to be washed out:

- **health problems** - hip dysplasia, vision or hearing loss, or a medical condition that can't be controlled.

- **aggression toward people or other dogs** - growling, barking, lunging, or other expressions of aggression are not acceptable in a service dog.

- **timid or fearful behavior** - the dog must be confident in new situations, reliable despite noises, children, or other environmental considerations.

- **specific behavioral problem you are unable to resolve** - for example jumping on people, barking, marking, easily distracted, i.e. common dog behaviors but not acceptable in an SD.

- **lack of ability or willingness to perform needed tasks safely and consistently** - this could be lack of mental capacity or desire, or physical, such as a person who needs mobility assistance and the dog doesn't grow as large as expected.

A lot of behavioral problems can be worked through, but some cannot. It's not always obvious when to pull the trigger and wash a dog. The advice of a professional trainer can provide crucial guidance when making this decision.

Sometimes it's the owner trainer who washes out. You may find yourself unable to keep up with training or unable to get assistance you need to train the dog. It happens.

A washed dog might remain in your home as a beloved pet, or you might decide the best option is to re-home it if you're going to begin over with a new prospect.

Sources for a Service Dog Prospect

There are three basic options for obtaining a prospect: a rescue, a breeder, or enlisting your current dog. The last is the least likely, as most family pets don't have an appropriate temperament for service dog work, but you can have your dog's temperament evaluated by a professional trainer if you think your dog is the exception. Also a pet that's more than a few years old won't have as many working years left by the time you're finished training it.

The biggest benefit of obtaining your dog from a breeder is that you will be able to meet the parents and see the environment the puppy was born into. These factors heavily impact how the dog turns out. A reputable breeder is also likely to provide health certifications and guarantees that you won't have to face hip dysplasia or other commonly inherited ailments a few years down the road. Purchasing a pure-bred dog from a quality breeder can be quite costly. It's worth asking the breeder if they would consider giving you a discount since you need the dog for service work. Breeders are occasionally willing to do so.

If you obtain your dog from a breeder or rescue organization, take care to read the fine print of any contract. Does the seller retain any control or partial ownership of the dog? A 30-day evaluation period is highly desirable, as the dog may not reveal its true nature immediately when thrown into a new environment. A dog that's been living in a foster home will be less traumatized than one from a shelter. A dog that seems shaky at first may just need some time to settle in to new surroundings, so don't panic if you get the dog home and it's afraid of the garage door opener or isn't acting as you anticipated. Give it time to adapt to its surroundings before deciding if there's a problem.

Puppy vs. Adult Prospect

You can start with a puppy or an adult dog, each has advantages. Many people like the idea of starting with a puppy. You get a clean slate, you know nothing bad has gone before, and there is nothing to undo. You get to bond with a puppy from the beginning. However, a puppy's temperament is not a guarantee of the temperament of the dog once it reaches maturity, so you're taking much greater risk of a washout.

Plus, puppies are a lot of work. They have to be housebroken, contained until they gain some sense, and monitored in a lot more detail. It will take 18 months to two years to make it to mature, full service dog. If you want a working service dog within a year, don't start with a puppy.

With a puppy, it's crucial that you ensure that the puppy is socialized intensively with other people and animals during the critical socialization period that occurs from eight to 17 weeks. If you have social anxiety that will prevent you from doing that, the chances of your puppy growing up to become a successful service dog are substantially lowered.

On the other hand, a suitable adult dog can potentially be trained in a much shorter time, especially if the dog already has some obedience training. You can more accurately assess whether it's friendly, okay with loud noises, food motivated, and free of potential issues such as resource guarding or anxiety. You may not be able to determine the dog's full past history, so there will be unknowns, and you will not have that puppy-bonding period where you get to know each other intimately, though ask anyone who has a rescue and you can rest assured that bonding closely with an adult dog is quite common. If you don't know the dog's parentage, it might be at greater risk for inherited medical issues than a dog whose lineage is known.

If you opt for an adult dog, experts recommend looking for an animal that is 18 months to 3-1/2 years old. In this range it will have reached mental maturity and still have most of its working life ahead.

The Started Dog Option

A "started dog" is an option worth investigating. Available in very limited quantities through breeders, started dogs are over a year old, thoroughly socialized, and have received basic obedience training. This can give you a significant jump start toward a working service dog. A started dog may be a washout from its originally intended career as a guide dog for the blind or other program, or specifically raised to be sold as a started dog. The show ring is a common source of these pups, as many fabulously pedigreed dogs fall short in some breed ideal such as not having specific proportions or the perfect coat color.

Selecting "The One"

Selecting an appropriate prospect is the most important decision you will make in this process. Do not rush this part! A solid prospect will have a suitable temperament for service dog work, have physical characteristics to perform the work you need, and be in excellent health. It's not the dog that's just like the one you had as a child, the dog that's going to be euthanized if you don't rescue it, or that giant fluffy breed you've always admired. Don't be distracted from your purpose - to find a prospect with the qualities and mental stability to successfully serve you as a working service dog for years to come.

It's a good idea to line up a professional trainer before you select your prospect, so that they can help you make a wise and informed choice. This will also increase the chances that you'll pick the most appropriate dog over the cutest one. Chapter 6: Working with a Professional Trainer provides advice on how to find a good trainer.

Identifying Suitable Breeds

There is no "best breed" for a psychiatric service dog. Breed selection should be made based on what you need the dog to do, your personality, personal preferences, and your living situation. Function is more important than form, and the breed that you think is best looking is likely to be different from the breed that will best serve you as a service dog. For example, if you suffer from severe anxiety, it's best to avoid breeds with a high protection/guard drive, such as German shepherds, Dobermans, or Rottweilers, as these dogs may respond to your anxiety by becoming aggressive, a big no-no in service dogs. Unusual breeds or breeds such as pit bulls may also increase the likelihood of access disputes or draw more unwanted attention, which can increase anxiety in some handlers.

Considering Size

One of the first considerations is size. If deep pressure therapy (DPT) is on your task list, then be sure to get a dog that's large enough to apply enough weight to make a difference. A 5-pound Chihuahua isn't going to be much use for DPT, although it might love to cuddle. At the other end, a very large dog like a St. Bernard would likely be too much, although you could train it to use just part of its body to apply pressure. A smaller dog is also easier to tuck away under a restaurant table or waiting room chair, a nice plus.

For many other PSD tasks, size isn't an issue. Any size dog can nudge or paw you to give an alert or distraction. A little dog won't be able to flip a light switch for you to light up the room, but it can activate a touch-lamp that's within its reach on the floor. Small dogs are easier to transport, cost less to feed, and tend to mature more quickly and have longer lifespans than large dogs. They also produce less poop. A medium or larger dog is likely to have an easier time retrieving medicine or an emergency phone for you.

If you will be using your dog for mobility or balance assistance in addition to psychiatric tasks, you need a bigger dog - 50 lbs or larger is recommended.

Factoring in Activity Level

All dogs need daily exercise, but some can get by with a lot less than others. A dog that needs more exercise than it gets is a dog that's likely to get into trouble and develop behavior problems. If you're a couch potato or live in a small apartment, the energy of a border collie is likely to overwhelm you. They are very smart dogs but they are rarely still! Greyhounds (a.k.a. the world's fastest couch potato) or Cavalier King Charles Spaniels are among the breeds considered to have a lower energy level. Golden retrievers and Labs fall in the middle of the scale. Although different breeds have characteristic energy levels, every dog is an individual.

Trainability is Key

The quality of being trainable or "biddable" is an important consideration. Breeds known for being particularly trainable include border collies, poodles, German shepherds, golden retrievers, and Labrador retrievers, among others. You can also assess candidates for this by giving them a mini training session (something as simple as sit or shake hands) to see how they react.

Coat Type Concerns

The type of coat your SD has matters for several reasons. It affects how much grooming will be required (and how much hair there will be collecting in the corners), and it also serves as a primary interface between you and your dog. If minimal maintenance is most important to you, pick a breed with a short, smooth coat, such as a greyhound. If you like a little more fluff with your snuggle, a medium or long coat may suit you better. Consider the amount of time and money you are willing and able to commit to brushing and grooming. A standard poodle, for example, will likely require regular trips to a professional groomer, while a Labrador retriever can usually be brushed out in five minutes. Although no dog is truly hypoallergenic, some, such as Schnauzers and poodles, come close, which can be a major blessing if you suffer from allergies.

Social Considerations

Do not dismiss social considerations when choosing a breed. Your dog's appearance will affect the amount of resistance (or lack of it) you receive as you move through your day. Say, for example, you have a thing for pit bulls. Perhaps you like their appearance and know several which are loving and intelligent. You might also be aware that some places have breed specific legislation (BSL) banning certain types of dogs, such as pit bulls, from occupying apartments or specific places. As a service dog, that ban would technically not apply, as under federal law a service dog can be any breed. On paper, it would seem you're good to go.

In the real world, however, you'd better be prepared to face additional obstacles brought on by your choice of dog. With a pit bull SD, you will be questioned more often, challenged more frequently, and stared at even more than you would be with, say, a golden retriever or Lab. You may face housing problems, because even though landlords must allow service dogs under the Fair Housing Act, they have an out - if the housing provider's insurance carrier would cancel or substantially increase the price of their insurance policy because of the presence of a certain breed of animal, such as a pit bull, that creates an "undue financial or administrative burden" on them, and they don't have to allow it. If you own your own home, you might have a similar problem through your home insurance provider.

Other breeds not typically associated with service work can add a little friction to your life as well, although some people actually like the extra attention and social interaction they can bring. Yes, these are things you can fight and usually work around, but will it be worth it? Which is more important to you, having a service dog or being a breed advocate?

Labrador retrievers and golden retrievers are often used for service work due to their size, temperament, and trainability. Many people are familiar with their use as service dogs. If you have social anxiety, one of these might be a good choice, as they will draw less attention and questioning than, for example, a Borzoi.

Mixed Breeds and Mutts

All this breed-selection talk might make you think that mixed breeds don't make good service dogs. That's not at all true- they can make exceptional service dogs. However it's a lot harder to predict the characteristics a mixed breed puppy will grow up to have, so the luck of the draw is going to play in a bit more. If your candidate is a mixed-breed adult, you can have it temperament tested. While puppies should also have an assessment, a dog's temperament can change as it matures, so a puppy test, while a worthwhile endeavour, is no guarantee of adult temperament. If you have access to the dog's parents, that can provide valuable clues, as temperament is often inherited.

Visual breed identification is startlingly inaccurate, even when performed by experts. So if someone tells you a dog is a particular breed and they're basing it on appearance rather than known parentage, don't count on it. In 2012, the University of Florida College of Veterinary Medicine asked nearly 6,000 self-identified dog experts (veterinarians, shelter staff, trainers, groomers, and the like) to identify the breed of 100 shelter dogs by looking at pictures of them and selecting their predominant breed from options on a drop-down list that included the correct answer and random options. To determine the correct answers, the dogs were genetically profiled to determine their actual breed components based on DNA.

Nearly a quarter of the dogs – 22 percent - had the correct breed chosen less than one percent of the time! Each of the dogs had an average of 53 different predominant breeds selected! Only 15 percent of the dogs were correctly identified more than 70 percent of the time. Clearly it is virtually impossible to correctly identify a mixed dog's breed by appearance alone, so keep that in mind when attempting to do so.

Need Help? There's an App for That!

You don't have to be a walking encyclopedia of dog breeds to figure out which come closest to matching your wish list, we have the internet for that. Try one or more of these online matchmakers:

- DogTime Dog Matchup (**dogtime.com/matchup**)

- Purina Breed Selector (**www.purina.com/dogs/dog-breeds**)

- Animal Planet Dog Breed Selector (**www.animalplanet.com/breed-selector/dog-breeds.html**)

Health Issues to Check Up On

Your prospect should undergo a thorough health screening by a licensed veterinarian, including all the standard checks for things like heart murmur, eye disorders, heartworm disease, and parasites. Many career-ending conditions are invisible to the naked eye but detectable by a veterinarian. The Orthopedic Foundation for Animals (OFA) maintains a list of genetic diseases and conditions associated with particular breeds. You can check the OFA (**www.ofa.org**) website to find out what genetic health screens are recommended for specific breeds.

Canine hip dysplasia (CHD) is a common, particularly insidious condition that can cripple a perfectly normal-appearing dog by middle age. With dysplasia, joints degenerate and become malformed, causing pain and progressive disability. It is the most commonly inherited orthopedic disease in dogs and afflicts more than 50 percent of dogs within some breeds. Adult dogs can be x-rayed to check for it. Although signs can sometimes be seen as young as 16 weeks, a dog can't be certified as clear until it has a clean x-ray at the age of two years old or older. For younger dogs, the best indicator is the parents' (and grandparents') status. There are two certification programs, OFA and AIS PennHIP, which are widely used as screening tools to help avoid this canine plague. If the dog is coming from a breeder, look for OFA or PennHIP certification on its bloodline. If you get a puppy prospect without one of these certifications on its parents, you're taking a big gamble.

Testing for Temperament

Faced with a half-dozen, roly-poly puppies, how can you tell which one would make the best service dog prospect? Is it the one who runs to you first? The one who watches you attentively but stays by mom? The one who ignores you completely and continues chasing a ball? The biggest?

Maybe you've been alerted to an adult dog that matches your criteria and has become available for adoption from a shelter or a breeder. How can you determine if it has a temperament and personality suitable for service dog work?

This is a key place where professional help can make or break your entire endeavour. A professional trainer, experienced with a large variety of dogs, can make a judgement by observing the dog and by putting it through an assessment designed to reveal its personality traits. This is called a temperament test. For guidance on finding a trainer to administer it, see Chapter 6: Working with a Professional Trainer.

Temperament tests can be a helpful tool for making these decisions. Temperament is defined as the combination of mental, physical, and emotional traits that describe the way an animal or person tends to behave most of the time. Temperament tests attempt to identify a particular individual's tendencies by assessing reactions to specific stimuli. The dog is put through a series of tests to assess traits such as confidence, prey drive, degree of dominance or submissiveness, stability, and independence. For example, most temperament tests will evaluate a dog's response to a loud, unexpected noise - does it flee, investigate, or ignore it? How long does it take for the animal to recover from the incident?

Temperament tests are a behavioral assessment tool, not a foolproof science. It's important to keep in mind that the results:

- ✓ reflect a snapshot in time - a specific response to a specific stimulus at a particular time in a specific environment. This response is used to predict the dog's behavior to a similar situation at a future point in time. Predictions are sometimes wrong.

- ✓ are most meaningful when administered by an experienced person to a dog living in a stable environment

- ✓ should be used in combination with other information, especially observations by the dog's previous owner and trained observers such as breeders, dog trainers, and experienced facility staff.

Although each test is a bit different, when used to screen a potential service dog, you are looking for a dog that is:

- ✓ Confident rather than timid

- ✓ People-oriented rather than independent

- ✓ Attentive to you rather than distracted by the environment

- ✓ Food and/or toy motivated - but not so focused on these things that they lose all focus on you

- ✓ Neither overly dominant nor overly submissive

- ✓ Calm rather than hyper, though this is partly a function of maturity

- ✓ For PSDs in particular, a dog that enjoys being touched and snuggled can be a big plus. Not all dogs are snugglers.

Don't lay everything on a single encounter - i.e. the test. Temperament is important, but it isn't everything. Socialization, training, and environment affect how that temperament will be manifested in everyday living.

A great deal of temperament is due to inherited genes, so meet the parents of your candidate if at all possible. Research shows personality is most consistently passed on to first-generation puppies of two pure-bred parents. When the parents are mixed breed, the inherited temperament tends to be less predictable, but the parents' personalities still have an effect.

Commonly Used Assessments

One of the most widely known temperament tests is the Volhard Puppy Aptitude Test (PAT). Many people have heard of this one, so if you bring it up with a breeder or trainer, they will be familiar with it (although they may have another they prefer). To give you a flavor for this and for temperament tests in general, here's a summary of the ten areas the Volhard PAT covers.

1) **Social Attraction** - Degree of social attraction to people

2) **Following** -Willingness to follow a person

3) **Restraint** -Assesses dominant or submissive tendency

4) **Social Dominance** - Degree of acceptance of social dominance (by person)

5) **Elevation** -Degree of accepting dominance while in position of no control

6) **Retrieving** - Degree of willingness to do something for you

7) **Touch Sensitivity** - Degree of sensitivity to touch

8) **Sound Sensitivity** - Sensitivity to sounds such as loud noises

9) **Sight Sensitivity** - Sensitivity to moving objects, such as squirrels

10) **Stability** - Response when confronted with a strange object

A test for each item is administered in the order above and the pup is assigned a score from one to six for each, depending on their response. The examiner can use the results to infer a dog's suitability for a particular purpose (i.e. service dog, police dog, family with children pet, etc.). To learn about the administration and interpretation of this particular test, visit **www.volhard.com**. This test is most meaningful when administered by someone who has done it many times and knows how to interpret the results. Trying to administer it yourself if you're inexperienced is not advisable.

Other commonly-used temperament tests include:

- **ATTS Temperament Test (www.atts.org)** - The American Temperament Test Society (ATTS) test is for dogs 18 months or older. A detailed description of the test is posted on the website.

- **ASPCA SAFER (www.aspcapro.org/safer)** - This assessment is primarily done in shelters to evaluate a dog's propensity toward aggression.

Do-it-Yourself Temperament Testing

Temperament testing is as much art as science, so it's much to your benefit to enlist a professional trainer to perform this critical task. If you absolutely must do it yourself, The Brown Aptitude Test for Service (BATS), developed by my go-to service dog trainer and handler Lindsay Brown with Paws Then Play LLC and detailed below, is highly recommended. To give this assessment:

- ✓ Bring an extra person to help, take notes, and be a distraction. Some shelter workers will do this for you but don't count on it.

- ✓ Execute each assessment listed on the BATS worksheet. Circle the result so that when you're done you can get an at-a-glance sense of the overall result.

- ✓ Make sure you know how to recognize signs of aggression (see sidebar) and stop the assessment immediately if any of them occur.

Doing well on a temperament test like this one is not a guarantee but it is a huge step in the right direction to help minimize risk of wash-out!

Brown Aptitude Test for Service (BATS)

Test	Ideal	Acceptable	Fail
Touch the dog gently all over, including back, belly, tail, ears, mouth, and toes. Grasp its feet.	Wags happily and kisses you on the nose. Loose body.	Stands, does not try to move away.	Moves away or shows any sign of aggression.
Test sound sensitivity by dropping a pan or using a windup toy or other things that would be new and unexpected.	Polite curiosity. Turns to look and notice it, looks towards you, no overt signs of fear.	Sniffs it, circling, approaching and sniffing. Stiff body or startles but recovers quickly.	Flattening to ground, cowering or hiding, whale eye (wide-open showing the whites).
Primary handler passes by other people with dog on leash. First person stands still. Next person perhaps tries to greet. Should be able to do with people and dogs.	Dog notices person but still follows the handler/person holding the leash. May glance/tail wag but moves with person.	Leash holder might have to urge dog or provide treats but dog will still move with leash holder.	Dog has to greet every person or dog they pass and/or drag person off their feet.
Engage dog with plush toy or tug rope or similar item. Get their interest, and then throw it.	Dog trots over picks it up and brings it back to you, doesn't necessarily give it to you.	Dog isn't interested in toy. Dog investigates and returns without item.	Dog mouths hand that threw it. Picks up thing and tries to shake it to pieces (this is prey drive) or takes it and tries to keep it from you.
Create a mild stress for the dog such as a light pinch along the side or pull gently on ears or tail.	Dog may duck head slightly but still stays close to you. It may lick you (a sign of submission).	Dog may back away from you but then returns, essentially forgiving you.	Vocalization. Any attempt to bite. Leaving and not wanting to come back.

Hold a high value treat in closed fist at dog's nose level for 15 seconds. (Give the treat afterward if no aggression).	Gentle nudges but then backs up and looks to handler, dog may offer a sit, dog does not try to pry treat from your hand.	Nudging, licking, even pawing a little bit at your hand.	Nipping at hand, rambunctious pawing or other aggressive attempts to get the food. Anything threatening.
Conduct a brief mini-training session. A basic lure into a sit or down position with a treat will work, if the dog doesn't already know these commands.	Willing to follow/engage/ easily trainable. Gives you the behavior.	Follows but does not give you the behavior.	Completely ignores or tries to snatch or nip to get food/toy.
Turn your back to the dog and ignore it.	Polite interest, then settles/relaxes.	Solicits attention from you politely.	Demands attention (jumping, barking, pawing).
Send the dog into a crate/kennel and close the door. If necessary, lure in by tossing a treat inside.	Dog willingly enters kennel, is comfortable with door closed for 3 minutes.	Lured in with treat, stays in without pawing or whining for 3 minutes.	Dog refuses to enter crate, even with treat, or enters and claws frantically, paces, pants, vocalizing.
Startle reflex and recovery: such as umbrella opening, mechanical/moving toy.	Looks but does not seem concerned. May lean in to sniff.	May flinch but recovers quickly. Single bark.	Freaks out! Big jump towards or away, vocalization, flattening to the ground, hides or shakes
Hug gently.	Leans into your arms.	Tolerates hug.	Attempts to escape.
Gently maneuver onto back and hold there. This is NOT an alpha roll.	Accepts being held. Lets you move its body into different positions.	Needs some verbal encouragement or reassurance and then will submit.	Begins to avoid person, wants to escape.

Danger! Warning signs of fear and aggression

Anyone who works with dogs should be able to read the signals they give off through behavior and body language, especially those related to fear or aggression, either of which can lead to a bite. Often it's obvious, but the signs can also be subtle and then suddenly the dog seems to explode from nowhere. You should reject a candidate that has fear or aggression issues. Even more important is to avoid getting bitten while assessing an unfamiliar candidate! If any of the following signs appear, stop the test immediately and consider the candidate unsuitable for service work:

- Dog becomes rigid and still, stares at you

- Excessive yawning or lip licking (a sign of nervousness - some is okay)

- Whale eye (showing whites of eyes)

- Panting when not hot

- Cowering

- Dog runs away from you and won't come back

- Trembles, tucks tail

- Snarls, growls, snaps, or lunges toward you or other obvious signs of aggression

- Lots of pacing/can't be still

While many dogs who display these signs can be rehabilitated with careful work, they do not make good service dog candidates. Remember, you are looking for a working partner, not a fix-it project!

Developing a Training Agenda

The Americans with Disabilities Act (ADA) does not specify specific obedience requirements for service dogs beyond that they must be housebroken and under the handler's control. In practice, however, service dogs need to have a high level of obedience training along with a sterling set of social manners, plus of course task-specific training. Reaching this level requires work in five primary areas:

1) **Socialization & Habituation:** The dog must be gradually introduced to a large variety of people and situations in careful, planned manner.

2) **Basic Obedience:** The dog should be well-versed in the standard commands every dog should know, including sit, lie down, stay, but trained to a higher standard of performance.

3) **Manners:** Service dogs must be masters of self-control while on duty. No sniffing shelves, eating tasty tidbits off the floor, or other "unprofessional" behavior.

4) **Public Access Skills:** The dog must be trained in how to behave in public spaces like restaurants, waiting rooms, the airport, or anywhere else your service dog may accompany you.

5) **Task Training:** The individualized work/tasks your dog will do to mitigate your disability must be trained.

You should have socialization and basic obedience in place before beginning public access training, but otherwise training for these areas doesn't have to be sequential. You can start task training before public access training or intermix different types of training. The important thing is that you have goals and a plan for reaching them. It's a good idea to use existing standardized tests to mark your progress. The AKC Canine Good Citizen (CGC) test is a good first target. It has 10 requirements:

1) **Accepting friendly stranger** - Dog accepts a friendly stranger approaching and speaking to handler

2) **Sitting politely for petting** - Dog allows a friendly stranger to approach and pet it

3) **Appearance and grooming** - Dog allows someone to check its ears and front feet

4) Walk on a loose lead

5) **Walk through a crowd** - Dog and handler pass close to several people (at least three)

6) Sit and down on command and stay

7) **Come when called** - from 10 feet, on leash

8) **Reaction to another dog** - Dog can behave politely around another dog

9) **Reaction to distraction** - Evaluator presents two distractions such as dropping something or sweeping with a broom. Dog may show slight startle but not run away, bark, or show fear.

10) **Supervised separation** - Evaluator takes hold of dog's leash and handler leaves for three minutes. Dog may show mild nervousness but may not bark, whine, etc.

There are additional levels of the CGC program. The AKC Urban CGC (CGCU) tests behavior in an urban setting, including navigating streets, buildings and doorways, and ignoring food on the sidewalk. The AKC Community Canine (a.k.a. advanced CGC or CGCA) is very similar to the CGC but adds a few extra hurdles and complications.

You can find a CGC evaluator near you through the AKC website (**www.akc.org/dog-owners/training/canine-good-citizen/finding-classes-evaluators/**).

Some people lay out a detailed training blueprint with daily goals and intricate detail, while others follow a less regimented approach and just take one or two goals at a time. Either way, it's a good idea to keep a training log documenting your progress. The log will help keep you on track and provide information to any professional trainer you might work with. There's another important reason to document your dog's training: if anyone ever challenges that your dog is a legitimate service dog, the training logs can be used as evidence to back up your claims. Some people also video record any tests they take along the way, such as the CGC or a public access test, for this reason.

Service dog training standards

Several groups have stepped forward to address this gap between what's specified in the ADA and what's really required of effective service dog teams by creating and promoting formal service dog training standards. Many trainers, both owner trainers and organizational trainers, look to these standards for guidance. The most widely known are:

- The International Association of Assistance Dog Partners (IAADP) Minimum Training Standards for Public Access (**www.iaadp.org**)

- Psychiatric Service Dog Partners (PSDP) Public Access Standard (**www.psychdogpartners.org**)

Each of these contains descriptions of how a service dog team is expected to behave in particular situations, such as entering a building, navigating a store, or while dining in a restaurant. PSDP also has a corresponding test, called a public access test (PAT), that you or someone else can use to assess if your dog meets the proposed standards.

Shaping Up Social Skills

Service dogs must be confident and stable in a great variety of situations and tolerant of a diverse range of people and animals. The foundation for this is laid in puppyhood, specifically between the ages of three weeks and four months. This is a critical window and if you miss out on it you cannot make up for it later! An older dog can still learn to accept new things, but it will be a lot harder.

Socialization is accomplished by introducing your dog to different environments, people, objects, animals, and sounds. It does not mean throw a leash and collar on your puppy and take it everywhere with you; that can be overwhelming and backfire, creating fear instead of confidence. Only introduce the pup to new things when you can control the experience. Make sure all interactions are positive and the puppy feels good about them. Don't force the puppy - if it wants to retreat, allow it. Keep the interactions short, a few minutes at a time is all that's needed. Here are some of the things you should introduce your dog to:

- ✓ Surfaces: Dirt, gravel, concrete, carpet, grates, sand, puddles

- ✓ People: Children, men and women of all sizes and races, people wearing hats or backpacks, people with medical equipment such as a cane or wheelchair, people in costumes and uniforms

- ✓ Animals: Dogs of different sizes, horses, cows, small animals, reptiles

- ✓ Objects: Umbrellas, balloons, vacuum

- ✓ Sounds: Fireworks, thunder, music, engines, barking dogs, babies crying

- ✓ Places: Vet office, boat, bowling alley, movie theatre, busses, dog shows

- ✓ Events: Car rides, street fairs, parties, sporting events, restaurant, mall

You will not be able to introduce your puppy to all of these things as a puppy. Stick to pet-friendly places for public outings until your pup has some basic obedience under his belt. Enrolling in puppy kindergarten provides a great opportunity for controlled socializing with other dogs and people.

Socialization should be maintained through adulthood. If your service dog is going places with you regularly, that will pretty much take care of itself.

Laying Obedience Foundations

It's a good idea to enroll your dog in group lessons ASAP and begin work on basic obedience skills at home as well. These foundation obedience skills are the groundwork that your service dog's real tasks will lay atop. You may be able to complete basic obedience training on your own or through inexpensive group lessons, but if you run into any trouble it's well worth investing in the assistance of a professional trainer. Dog training is as much about training the owner as it is about teaching the dog. You must learn how to handle the dog just as much as the dog must learn to perform particular behaviors on command. It's a partnership that requires both sides in order to work.

There is nothing special about these obedience basics. Any dog benefits from knowing these items, though with a service dog they become crucial rather than simply desirable. There's a bountiful supply of books, web sites, and professional trainers poised to help you work through them. The book *Teamwork, Book 1,* is particularly good.

Your basic obedience plan will need to include:

- ✓ Walking on a loose leash, remaining at your side

- ✓ Solid sit-stay and down-stay, even with distractions present

- ✓ Coming when called

- ✓ Leave it - if you tell the dog to ignore something (like a dropped piece of food) he should do so.

- ✓ Housetraining

These are everyday basics you can learn from any dog training book or class.

Minding Service Dog Manners

Service dogs are ideally unobtrusive, melting into the background unless they need to step forward and perform a task. One of the favorite compliments a service dog handler can receive is for someone to spot the dog and say "I didn't even know a dog was in here!"

This means they have to learn to control some of their natural tendencies, and developing these skills should be part of your training plan:

- ✓ Ignoring food on the floor or otherwise within reach

- ✓ Potty on command (so you can ensure it's done in an appropriate place)

- ✓ No soliciting petting or attention from other people while on duty

- ✓ No aggressive behavior toward other people or animals

- ✓ No sniffing or mouthing of merchandise when walking down an aisle or standing in line, etc.

- ✓ Going under - dog goes out of the way beneath a chair or table and lies down and stays there

- ✓ Tucking - dog lies down and curls up into a compact position, with tail tucked

- ✓ Waiting at thresholds - dog should wait for your permission to cross a threshold, including getting into or out of a car or going out your front door

Practicing Public Access Skills

Federal law gives access rights to people with trained service dogs only, not people with dogs still in training. Yet teaching your dog some of these things requires taking them in public to do so. It's kind of a catch-22 situation, but there are ways to work around it.

In any case, start public access practice at pet-friendly venues, such as pet stores and other establishments that welcome pets. Some outdoor cafes allow dogs in patio seating areas. These are ideal places to start because people will be more understanding (and you'll be less embarrassed) if undesirable behavior happens.

Many states recognize this public access conundrum and address it by giving service dogs in training the same access granted to full service dogs, specifically for training purposes. If you live in one of them, you're good to go. If not, check neighboring states. It's not ideal, but crossing state lines to work on public access training might be your best option. Otherwise, your public access training options are limited and you're basically limited to pet-friendly venues until your dog meets the criteria to be considered a full-fledged service dog. In some states a professional trainer may be allowed to work with your SDiT in public places even if you can't.

In any case, don't bring your brand new, untrained prospect to the grocery store to "socialize" them or begin public access work. Before beginning public access practice, your SDiT should have basic obedience skills down solidly. Ideally, they should be able to pass the AKC Canine Good Citizen test (even if you opt not to actually take it). There's no rush to get started on public access until the time is appropriate.

Individualized Work & Task Training

Everything on the training agenda so far is foundational work that is largely the same for any service dog. All that stuff is crucial, but it's really just a supportive framework for the magic of the matter - tasks and work that address your individual disabilities and make your life better on a daily basis. Hopefully you have a pretty detailed list in mind after reading Chapter 3: Is a Service Dog Right for You.

While you should start immediately on socialization, basic obedience, and public access skills, you don't have to wait until those things are rock solid to begin task training - it can proceed in parallel. Prioritize the items and begin work on them. If DPT (deep pressure therapy) is on your list, that's a great place to start. The book *Teamwork II: A Dog Training Manual for People with Disabilities* may be helpful. It isn't specific to psychiatric service dogs and focuses on mobility tasks such as retrieving up dropped items rather than covering PSD tasks such as DPT, but it gives great advice on different ways tasks can be trained and is valuable as on overall task training guide.

Linking Up with a Trainer

Owner training does not have to mean alone-training. How closely you work with a dog trainer is a matter of personal preference, budget, and access. Most people who start with an appropriate dog and are willing to work at it are capable of training their own psychiatric service dog, especially now that there are so many wonderful resources available online, such as free dog training videos on YouTube. You might be okay completely on your own using these resources, but it's also possible you'll need to turn the majority of the work over to a professional who does this for a living.

Many owner trainers take a middle road. They carry out some training themselves but seek out structured, formal assistance for specific aspects through private training or group classes.

Finding a suitable trainer is an important task best addressed before you even obtain your candidate dog. A trainer with service dog experience would be ideal, but there aren't very many of those around. Fortunately, the principles that apply to other types of dog training are completely relevant to training a psychiatric service dog. Much of what is needed is strong basic obedience and public manners, with specialized tasks and work added on top. As long as you can specifically define what you need, any competent and willing trainer can help you achieve it.

Chapter 6 details the process of finding and working with professional dog trainers.

Keeping a Training Log

Although it's not absolutely critical, there are several good reasons to take the time to keep a training log of your team's progress. A log will help you keep track of your progress and remember where you are in your overall plan. You might not think you'd need such a reminder, but in owner training it frequently happens that the owner trainer has to interrupt training due to personal difficulties or life interfering and then pick it up again when the situation allows. It's easy for details to slip out of your mind at times like these, and the log can help bring them back.

As you progress, you'll also discover that you've covered a whole lot of ground. Dogs need to review previously learned commands in order to retain them over time. With a training log, you can more certainly run through the list and be certain you're not leaving anything out.

Last but not least, although it's unlikely you'll ever find yourself in a courtroom defending your dog's standing as a service dog, it could happen. Your log can serve as evidence of the training your dog has received to make it a service dog.

Figure 5-1: Sample Training Log

Service Dog Training Log
Date: _____ Location: _____ Time spent: _____
Trainer: _____

Behavior(s):

Target Goals:

Performance:

Comments:

Health Notes:

The log can take any format that suits you. Figure 5-1
demonstrates a possible format. Some people keep a daily log
while others summarize things on a weekly basis. Information to
track includes:

- ✓ hours spent on training

- ✓ number and types of outings

- ✓ obedience commands that you worked on, where you
  worked on them, and how your dog performed (noting any
  problems)

- ✓ socialization training, such as exposing the dog to a new
  environment

- ✓ service tasks worked on and how well the dog is performing
  them

- ✓ health notes

✓ a comments section where you can detail your thoughts on this training period and note any special accomplishments or concerns

Graduating to Full Service Dog Status

The point when your dog can legally qualify as a service dog and the time you choose to graduate your canine partner to that status may not be the same. From a strictly legal definition (in the U.S), if your dog is trained to perform at least one task that mitigates your disability, then it's a service dog. It doesn't have to be a master of good behavior, ace public access, or be a virtual Swiss army knife of tasks to meet this legal definition. The dog does have to be potty trained and successfully under your control to be able to go into public places with you. If these things are true, you can call your dog a service dog and be legally accurate, whether or not it knows how to tuck, stay despite distractions, or ignore other dogs.

However, most owner trainers strive for a higher standard and do not graduate their dog to full service dog status until they have reliable obedience performance under a variety of conditions in addition to performing tasks. Keeping that "in training" patch on your dog's vest a little longer can be a bit like a security blanket - you don't feel quite so embarrassed if your partner breaks training and acts unprofessional. There's no rush to "go pro" unless your state is one that does not allow service dogs in training public access rights and you need them.

The International Association of Assistance Dog Partners (IAADP) Minimum Training Standards for Public Access is a valuable yardstick for determining when your dog is ready to graduate from SDiT to SD. Psychiatric Service Dog Partners also maintains a detailed public access standard and companion exam that can be used for this purpose. Both offer detailed lists of training level and behavior expected of service dogs. You can use PSDP's companion public access test (PAT) to determine if you and your dog are ready to make the leap to full service dog. Assistance Dogs International (ADI) publishes a public access test as well, but it's primarily geared toward use by ADI member organizations, not owner trainers. You can find these standards on each organization's website.

A PAT is used and talked about by so many in the service dog community that you might think it's a requirement, but it's not, it's only a very useful option. Owner trainers who take a PAT sometimes choose to record the effort on video to document their canine partner's performance level. Even if you don't take a formal PAT, you should familiarize yourself with the standards offered by each of these organizations and use them to help define your training plan and goals.

If you opt to owner train, you will be taking on a major challenge that will continue for months or even years. During that time you will become frustrated at your dog's backsliding periods, wonder if you should wash your dog out, question whether you yourself are really capable of doing this, and in the best moments, feel elated at your achievements. Owner training a service dog is definitely not right for everyone, but many people can pull it off with great success. The best way to ensure that you can be one of them is to do your research up front, choose your candidate dog carefully, immerse yourself in the facts and details of dog training and service dog ownership, and be persistent and stick with it for the long run. Connecting with other owner trainers and sharing progress and plans can be a big help. Chapter 8: Getting to Know the Service Dog Community can help with this.

Chapter 6

Working with a Professional Trainer

In This Chapter

➢ Tracking down a quality dog trainer

➢ Recognizing different training techniques

➢ Assessing trainer credentials and experience

➢ What to expect in a training contract

➢ Choosing between group classes, private lessons, and board & train

More owner trainers than not work with a trainer either individually or in group classes at some point. Some people opt to locate and connect with a trainer before even choosing a prospect, so that the trainer can assist them with the selection. Others take advantage of professional advice on a periodic basis, depending on their personal training skillset and budget. It's true that signing on with a trainer can run up quite a bill over time, but if it means you end up with a working dog instead of a washout, it's well worth it.

Unfortunately, finding the right trainer can be a little tricky. Dog training is an unregulated industry, with no standard licensing or certification required. Anyone can hang up a sign (or publish a fancy web site) and proclaim himself or herself a dog training expert. Associations and certification programs abound, but the standards are all over the place so you can't assume an official sounding title is as meaningful as it appears. There are many accomplished and even gifted trainers, but there are also plenty of hacks, inexperienced people, and trainers with outdated skillsets - it's up to you to assess competence and fit. Good dog trainers are often found through connections, so try these sources:

- ✓ Ask friends and relatives for recommendations

- ✓ Ask local rescue groups who they work with

- ✓ Ask a trusted veterinarian or groomer

- ✓ If you encounter a well-behaved dog, ask the owner who trained it

Once you get some names, Google them. A trainer's website can tell you a lot about their personality and training ideology. Do you like what they have to say? Often details of their training and experience will be spelled out on their website.

Next, get the trainer on the phone. Ask about their training and experience (even though you read it on their website, it's good to hear it straight from the source). Ask them about their own dog(s). If they don't have any, be wary. It's unusual for a dog trainer to be dogless. Usually they will have one or more dogs and those dogs will have some kind of obedience titles, such as CDX (AKC Companion Dog Excellent) or something else. If you like what you hear, ask for references and set up a time to see the trainer in action. Then you can observe the methods they use and consider whether you are comfortable using them, too. Things to look for include:

- ✓ Are handlers and dogs comfortable or looking stressed?

- ✓ Does the trainer explain what they are doing?

- ✓ Although there are exceptions, most often puppies and adult dogs should be in separate classes

- ✓ Look for a focus on reward-based training. Rewards can be treats, play, toys, or praise.

If you see any leash popping or striking, go elsewhere. Ditto alpha rolling (aggressively rolling the dog on its back) or shaking the dog by the scruff.

Recognizing Training Styles

The field of dog training is constantly evolving and there are a variety of techniques that can be employed. Be prepared to encounter a bounty of opinions about which are good, bad, terrible, or "the best." People can be very fanatical about the methodology they feel is best, verbally skewering anyone who dares to differ. However, as with so many things, there really is more than one acceptable answer, so don't fall into the "there's only one right way" trap. The right way is a way that you feel comfortable with and, most importantly, that works for your particular dog and its training needs.

Reward-focused training is currently enjoying wide popularity over training that employs compulsive or aversive methods. A focus on the positive seems to work well for dogs and their handlers and it's something you can feel good about while working with your prospect. Some trainers take this to the maximum level, with no negative consequences or corrections of any kind, ever, and are certain that is the only humane way to train.

When considering where you feel comfortable on this spectrum, keep in mind that negative consequences don't have to be cruel or abusive to be effective and rewards can take many forms. For example, simply turning your back to a dog and ignoring it briefly is a negative reinforcer. So is a sharply formed "no."

Rewards are tailored to the dog and the circumstance and may change over time depending on the point in training. Reward often means a tasty treat, but it can also be praise, play, a favorite toy, or something else that a particular dog values. Some dogs will do almost anything for a session of tug while others have zero interest in such silliness but will stand on their head for a nibble of peanut butter. Over time, as the behavior becomes solid, the reward is gradually phased out. If you're not comfortable applying a training method or using particular equipment yourself, then you should not work with a trainer who uses it.

There was a brief period where emphasis on asserting and maintaining dominance and a "leader of the pack" position enjoyed popularity, but it has since been disproved as a general use training methodology. If a trainer you are considering promises to teach you to become "leader of the pack," find a different one quickly!

Ask potential trainers:

- ✓ **What methods do you use?** The trainer should use a variety of methods so they can switch between them depending on what works for the dog in a particular situation. Luring and shaping are examples of training methods.

- ✓ **Do you have particular equipment you recommend?** Trainers use a variety of equipment, including different types of collars. The choice of equipment should always be tailored to each individual dog's disposition and training status and may change as the dog progresses. Certain tools, such as prong collars (also called pinch collars), are reserved for very specific needs, so if the trainer pulls one out right off the bat, that's generally a bad sign, kind of like swatting a fly with a baseball bat. Stim collar is a euphemism for shock collar and you probably don't want to go there for basic service training. Flat collars, head halters, and harnesses are all acceptable.

- ✓ **How do you handle it if a dog doesn't do what you want it to?** Try a different approach would be a great answer here, while throw a shake can (a can that makes a loud noise) or apply a leash pop correction would be an indication the trainer favors aversive techniques over reward methods. I do nothing, because I use reward-based training is another acceptable answer, if you're open to the reward-only route.

Deciphering the lingo

When you ask a trainer what sort of methodologies they use, you're likely to get some terminology back in return. Words that may get thrown your way include:

Luring - Using a treat to entice the dog into the desired position, such as a sit.

Shaping - Building a new behavior by rewarding small, incremental steps toward it. For example, to teach your dog to hold something in its mouth, you might first reward for looking at the object. When it does so consistently, up the ante so the dog must move toward the object to receive the reward, then touch the object, then mouth the object in any way, then take the object in its mouth, then hold it.

Capturing - Catching the dog in the act of performing a desired behavior, such as sitting, and rewarding for the behavior. This is repeated until the dog reliably makes the connection between the behavior and the reward.

Cue - A signal that indicates to a dog that it should perform a behavior. This could be a hand signal, a word, a behavior, or an environmental change the dog can observe.

Correction - An action that punishes a dog for performing an undesirable behavior or prevents it, for example a sharp "NO!" or a leash jerk.

Positive Reinforcement - Giving the dog something that rewards the behavior, such as a treat or playtime with a favorite toy.

Clicker Training - A clicker is a small noisemaker that a trainer uses to precisely mark a desired behavior. The dog is first trained to associate the sound the clicker makes with a treat. Then the clicker is used to signal quickly and clearly to the dog that they have performed a desired behavior. Once the behavior is learned, the clicker is phased out. A verbal marker, such as "YES!" can be used in place of an actual clicker. This is an application of operant conditioning theory.

Socialization - Introducing a dog to new things *while taking care that the dog feels successful and enjoys the experience*. The second part is the key to successful socialization.

There are many more terms associated with dog training, and if a trainer throws one at you that you don't understand, simply ask for an explanation, which they should be happy to provide.

Considering Education and Certifications

When you begin your search for professional help, you'll quickly encounter an expansive array of professional titles and business cards splattered with bewildering collections of letter combinations. This is primarily a reflection of the fact that there are many routes to a career as a dog trainer, along with many philosophies of training. Some trainers have formal education from a vocational program or college, while others come into the field through an apprenticeship process or through working in animal shelters; most have a background that includes both education and personal experience.

With all of these possibilities, if your potential trainer doesn't have any letters at all after their name, don't panic. A professional partakes of formal programs to build their professional toolset, but they may not list all of these things everywhere their name appears.

When checking out credentials, you'll encounter both certificates and certifications. Certificates are obtained by satisfactorily completing an educational program. Certifications are earned by passing a knowledge and/or hands-on skills assessment and aren't associated with a particular education program. Sometimes they include additional requirements such as meeting experience criteria or supplying references. The term certification is commonly used incorrectly, however, when the credential is really a certificate.

There are "credentials" that can be earned simply by paying a fee and completing a minimal online course, so you'll want to take the time to look up the ones being presented to you. It's easy enough with an internet connection - go to a library if you don't have one at home. One legitimate designation you'll run into quite often is CPDT-KA (Certified Professional Dog Trainer-Knowledge Assessed) which comes from Certification Council for Professional Dog Trainers. Once again, it's generally a positive indicator but no guarantee on its own - you must assess the full picture of education, experience, and references in addition to credentials. It's also just one of many possible options.

Membership in professional associations can be a good sign also, but don't pin too much on it. The trainer might use the association as a way to help keep up on the latest training trends and learn about education opportunities, or their only involvement might be paying annual dues.

Assessing Professional Experience

Identify how much and what sort of experience the trainer has actually working with dogs. This information is likely available on their website but don't hesitate to ask if you need to fill in any blanks. Have they taught primarily group lessons or worked with clients one-on-one? The more experience in the type of training you're seeking, the better, but that's also going to ratchet up the cost, and in some areas trainers with extensive experience aren't available, so don't automatically cross a trainer off your list if they don't have decades of hands-on training under their belt. However, don't sign on with anyone who has less than a full year of experience working as a trainer (not as an apprentice). That might be okay for a pet learning basic obedience, but not for a future service dog.

Contract Matters

If you're planning an extended engagement with a particular trainer, a contract is a good thing to have. Signing a training contract can seem scary, especially if it's heavily decorated with words in all caps, which many are. There's no need to be intimidated though; a contract protects both you and the trainer. A good one spells out expectations for both sides. It should describe the services the trainer will provide and what the training goals are, along with a time frame, cost, and method of payment.

It may also state that your consistent participation is a requirement for obtaining a successful outcome. This is a good reminder for you that that no matter how great the trainer is, you must practice with the dog and follow the instructions given by the trainer or you're not going to end up with a trained dog.

Don't be disturbed by a disclaimer along the lines of, "Trainer will make every reasonable effort to attain training goals but makes no guarantee. " Animals are individual and unpredictable and it's not possible to guarantee outcomes. In fact, if the trainer offers a "100% guarantee" that's a red flag and not a good thing!

A liability waiver (alternatively called "release of liability") will be in there as well, and this often contains the most capital letters. While on the surface it will seem to say you have no legal recourse no matter what happens, most states make it against public policy to contract away gross negligence. So in the unlikely event the trainer does something truly egregious, there's a good likelihood you can still sue, although not always.

Many contracts contain a clause about dispute resolution and/or contract termination. This is another good thing to know up front - if you are unhappy with something about the training, what is the policy for handling that?

Some contracts, especially from corporations like big-box pet stores, will seem excessively long and detailed. It's still best to spend the time to read through them just to ensure the terms are as agreed and there are no hidden surprises.

Additional things to ask, which might not be in the contract but are important to know, include:

- ✓ Can I call or email you between lessons and is there a charge for that? Some consider this a built-in while a few will charge per-instance.

- ✓ Do you have liability insurance?

- ✓ What if the training doesn't succeed in the specified time? Is there a discount on retakes? This mostly applies to group classes.

You can ask for something to be added to the contract if it's not included. In addition, you can always have a contract reviewed by an attorney (at your cost, of course) before you sign. Obviously you're not going to do that for a $75 group obedience class but you might if you're agreeing to pay $4,000 for comprehensive service dog training. File your copy somewhere you can find it again, just in case.

Selecting a Training Format

Training may be delivered in a group setting or in private, one-on-one sessions. Private lessons are usually priced per session, while group classes are usually sold in packages of a series of sessions. A third option is board and train, where the dog lives at the training facility for a period of time, often one or two weeks, and receives intensive training while there. All of these formats have benefits, and which you use should be a matter of preference and budget.

When working with a trainer, either individually or in a group class setting, the flow commonly goes something like this: The trainer introduces a new behavior to the dog (such as lie down). Then the trainer instructs you on how to elicit the behavior, as well as what to do if your dog misses the boat, either through innocent misunderstanding or deliberate refusal. From there it's up to you to practice and proof the behavior in different situations (i.e. do your homework).

Group Classes

Available through pet stores, training centers, and private trainers, group classes have a lot going for them, including:

- ✓ They are the most budget friendly in per-lesson cost.

- ✓ Your dog can interact with other people and dogs during the class, building critical social skills.

- ✓ It provides an opportunity for your dog to learn to accept handling by other people.

- ✓ There's plenty going on, giving your dog practice responding to you despite distractions.

- ✓ You will learn additional things by observing how other handlers and their dogs interact and work through obstacles.

- ✓ You get to meet other handlers and potentially form new friendships.

✓ Research shows that some dogs learn to some extent by watching as well as by doing!

Group classes typically include dogs that are close to each other in training level. For puppies, group classes provide an invaluable opportunity to learn how to behave and focus around other dogs. Don't be surprised if you find a new friend or two before the class is over.

Group classes are most useful for learning standard obedience commands at both basic and advanced levels. It's also a good setting for specialty training such as learning dog sports like agility and flyball or trick training. The fact that lessons come in packages and occur at regularly scheduled times can help keep you on track and moving forward. At the same time, the pre-set, controlled pace and curriculum may feel constraining if you have a quick learner.

Most group classes have a vaccination policy and will require evidence of current vaccinations before you can participate.

Private Lessons

The biggest benefit of one-on-one lessons is focus - it's all about you and your dog and what's next on *your* agenda. They can be more convenient than group classes because you have greater control over the schedule. A lesson can take place at your home, at the trainer's facility, or at another location chosen for a specific training purpose. This concentration and control does come at a cost, as private lessons typically cost 30 to 50 percent more than group lessons. On the other hand, you may progress much faster and need fewer lessons.

Privates are particularly good for working on specific issues, such as task training or ironing out a behavioral problem.

Board & Train

This is the boot camp of dog training. The dog resides (i.e. is boarded) at the training facility or the trainer's home, where it is given regular training sessions and taught new commands and behaviors. This might be one-on-one training, group training with other dogs, or a combination. The boarding period is often two weeks, but may be as long as four. This format can allow a trainer to more clearly communicate concepts so the dog can absorb more quickly and thoroughly.

When your dog comes home, it will arrive fully trained with the new skills, but you must still practice and reinforce them yourself. Essentially the trainer adds the skillset and then you reinforce it. There will likely be a follow-up session or two to train you on how to work with your dog's wonderful new repertoire. Depending on your dog's status and your needs, multiple board and trains may be required to meet your goals.

Board and train requires extreme trust on your part, because you will not even be present during the training period or witness how your dog is treated during and between sessions. It's important for you to understand what methods the trainer will use and be comfortable with them. You must recognize the importance of being consistent with follow-up practice for this to work; without practice the new skills may quickly fade.

This is the most expensive training format, costing from hundreds to thousands of dollars depending on the trainer and length of the session. It can be appealing and convenient to have someone else do most of the work, but be certain to do your homework and ensure you are sending your dog to a quality, established trainer. Check multiple references; one is not enough.

Things to keep in mind:

- ✓ Clarify if it will it be an in-home board and train where your dog will live with the trainer and be part of the family or kennel board and train where the dog will be kept in a kennel/crate when not receiving training – in- home is better.

- ✓ Be wary of any term less than two weeks. Two weeks gives your dog time to adjust to being in a new environment and be ready to learn. Animals cannot cram like people do and need time to get settled and acclimated. A three-day crash course is a bad idea because it is likely to do more harm than good due to the stress placed on the dog.

✓ Ensure there will be at least one session with you, the trainer, and your dog after the board and train to work with you on the new skills your dog has learned.

All of these training formats provide value, and you may choose to use different ones at different points in your dog's training. Although you could attempt to train your dog completely independently, unless you have substantial experience working with and training dogs with a variety of temperaments, you'll probably be setting yourself up for failure. Even if you have to limit your access to professional training due to budget constraints, don't write it off entirely. Ending up with a washout will ultimately be more expensive and heartbreaking than what you might spend on training.

Chapter 7

Knowing Service Dog Laws

In this chapter

➢ Why certification and registration aren't necessary

➢ Getting to know the Americans with Disabilities Act (ADA)

➢ Introducing The Rehab Act, a.k.a. Section 504

➢ Taking a service dog to grade school or college

➢ Where state laws come in

➢ Service animals in no-pets housing

➢ Taking to the friendly skies with your service dog

➢ Complaining to the right people, when necessary

➢ Taking a tax deduction for service dog expenses

Navigating United States laws pertaining to service dogs can get a little tricky, but as long as you remember that different laws cover different things, you'll be able to sort it out. This chapter was created to help with that. It isn't intended to be an exhaustive guide to all laws that might apply in every situation but covers the most common scenarios. It also isn't intended as legal advice and shouldn't be considered as such. If you need that, contact an attorney. If you just want information about laws affecting service dog teams, you're in the right place.

There are both federal and state laws that pertain to service dogs. Federal laws apply at a national level, which means they apply to the whole country and affect every state. Individual states can have their own service dog regulations as well, and some do. The federal laws take precedence but state laws can add additional regulations on top that must be adhered to in that state. State laws cannot overrule the federal laws, so if they conflict, federal law wins and is the one you (and the state) must follow. None of these laws pertains outside of the U.S., so when travelling internationally you'll need to research the applicable laws at your destination.

It's important to understand that service dogs don't have any legal rights; it's the disabled people handling the service dogs who have them. So it's your rights, not your dog's rights, that are explored in this chapter. This chapter focuses on the laws, but for tips and advice about managing outings and travel with your service dog, read Chapter 10: Out and About with Your Service Dog.

Access to public places, flying, and housing are each affected by separate laws. Table 7-1 summarizes which laws apply when.

Table 7-1: Sorting Through Service Dog Laws

Application	*Law*
Provides legal definition of service animal and specifies who is eligible to have one.	Americans with Disabilities Act (Title III)
Grants public access rights to service dog teams.	Americans with Disabilities Act (Titles II and III)
Requires employers to consider allowing an employee with a disability to use a service animal at work as a reasonable accommodation.	Americans with Disabilities Act (Title I)
Controls access rights with a service dog in training (SDiT) and may have additional effects.	Individual state laws

Requires service dogs to be permitted even in no-pets-allowed housing.	Applicable law depends on the type of housing, and is either the Fair Housing Act, the Rehabilitation Act of 1973, or the Americans with Disabilities Act.
Permits disabled individuals to be accompanied by their service animals in the plane's cabin when flying.	Air Carrier Access Act (ACAA)

You don't need a prescription from a physician or medical professional to have a service dog and benefit from these laws. You may, however, need documentation for certain purposes, such as requesting a reasonable accommodation at work, living in no-pets housing, or flying with a service animal. These situations and the relevant laws are discussed in detail below. There's also a collection of sample letters provided in Appendix B, and Appendix C lists tips for medical professionals who write them.

No Certification or Registration Required

There is no legal certification, registration, or special license required for service dogs in the United States. There are plenty of places that will sell you either one of those, but legally they mean nothing, so don't be fooled by official sounding "registries". The only exception is that some states offer voluntary service dog registration that applies to just that state. Your state cannot require you to register because the ADA says it can't. The state registration is a completely optional thing to do, and it's totally up to you whether you register or not. Doing so will not grant or remove any of the rights accorded to you under the ADA or other federal laws.

This doesn't mean that you are exempt from standard local license requirements that apply to all dogs in your area. If local regulations require all dogs to be licensed, your service dog must be licensed as well. Some places will waive the dog license fee for service dogs. Municipalities that offer to waive such fees can limit the offer to specific types of service dog or require documentation from you without violating the ADA.

Your service dog doesn't have to wear a vest, ID, or otherwise be externally identified as a service dog. Putting a vest on your dog can save you a lot of potential aggravation, but it's not required and there's no "official" vest. Some handlers choose to work their dog naked, as is their legal right, but most do dress it in a service dog vest because that helps avoid unwanted interactions.

The Americans with Disabilities Act

The Americans with Disabilities Act (ADA) is a federal law that prohibits discrimination against individuals with disabilities. It's essentially an equal rights law for people with disabilities. It is a comprehensive and complex law with many parts, but the sections that apply to service dog handlers are pretty clearly spelled out in supplementary documentation created by the U.S. government. The main things this legislation does for service dog handlers are:

- ✓ Providing a legal definition of disability

- ✓ Providing a legal definition of service animal

- ✓ Specifying who can have a service animal

- ✓ Setting forth the legal regulations that provide for service animals to accompany people with disabilities almost everywhere members of the public are allowed to go

The ADA has been revised several times. It was most recently revised in 2010, when changes were made to regulations related to service animals. You can attempt to decipher the legalese in the full act, which is available via the ADA website (**www.ada.gov**), but it's much more useful to head straight to the companion explanatory documents that spell out the important highlights in plain English. The most useful of these are included in the Appendix A. The key elements are also explained in this chapter.

You don't need to be an expert on the ADA to benefit from it, but it's never detrimental to be well-informed. The ADA is comprised of five sections, or Titles. Title I requires equal employment opportunities for individuals with disabilities. Title II applies non-discrimination rules to state and local governments and their programs and services, and Title III covers places of public accommodation. These are the three sections of most interest to service dog handlers. Title IV relates to telecommunications, such as closed captioning and TTY. Title V includes miscellaneous provisions. There is the Act itself, which sets forth requirements, and there are regulations that implement its requirements. Technically they are not the same thing, but when someone says "The ADA says" they could be referring to one or the other. This book doesn't distinguish between them, either.

Different government agencies received the responsibility for creating regulations for particular Titles. Title I is regulated and enforced by the Equal Employment Opportunity Commission (EEOC). Titles II and III are regulated and enforced by the U.S. Department of Justice.

Qualifying to Have a Service Animal

The ADA spells out key definitions relevant to the Act. The definitions of disability and of service dog are the two of primary interest to service dog handlers. You and your dog must adhere to both in order to be covered by the ADA.

Defining Disability

Since only people with disabilities are covered by the ADA, one of the first things the Act does is provide a legal definition of the term disability. You must meet this definition to be covered by the ADA and to legally qualify to have a service dog. It's actually pretty broad. Essentially, you must have a physical or mental impairment, and it must be an impairment that substantially limits one or more of your major life activities.

Here's the relevant text from the ADA:

(1) Disability

The term "disability" means, with respect to an individual

(A) a physical or mental impairment that substantially limits one or more major life activities of such individual;

(B) a record of such an impairment; or

(C) being regarded as having such an impairment (as described in paragraph (3)).

(2) Major Life Activities

(A) In general

For purposes of paragraph (1), major life activities include, but are not limited to, caring for oneself, performing manual tasks, seeing, hearing, eating, sleeping, walking, standing, lifting, bending, speaking, breathing, learning, reading, concentrating, thinking, communicating, and working.

(B) Major bodily functions

For purposes of paragraph (1), a major life activity also includes the operation of a major bodily function, including but not limited to, functions of the immune system, normal cell growth, digestive, bowel, bladder, neurological, brain, respiratory, circulatory, endocrine, and reproductive functions.

The ADA doesn't specifically name all impairments that are covered, but mental health impairments are specifically included, even those that are episodic in nature and come and go. You don't have to be unable to work or receiving Social Security disability benefits to be considered disabled under the ADA, nor do you need a note from a physician stating that you're disabled. Remember though, you can't meet this definition automatically just because you have a mental health impairment - it must be significant enough to substantially limit your participation in daily life.

Since the EEOC is responsible for implementing the employment-related provisions of the ADA, it has published a lot of information about it. One of the publications is a government FAQ titled

"Questions and Answers on the Final Rule Implementing the ADA Amendments Act of 2008" that lists "examples of specific impairments that will be easily concluded to substantially limit a major life activity," a list which includes major depressive disorder, bipolar disorder, post-traumatic stress disorder, obsessive-compulsive disorder, and schizophrenia.

There are a few things that the ADA specifies don't qualify as disabilities:

1) transvestism, transsexualism, pedophilia, exhibitionism, voyeurism, gender identity disorders not resulting from physical impairments, or other sexual behavior disorders;

2) compulsive gambling, kleptomania, or pyromania; or

3) psychoactive substance use disorders resulting from current illegal use of drugs.

If you're still in doubt, Google the document titled "EEOC Enforcement Guidance on the Americans with Disabilities Act and Psychiatric Disabilities" for more discussion on when a mental illness is considered a disability under the ADA. It's a bit on the old side (from 1997) but is still one of the best explorations available of when a psychiatric condition reaches the level of a disability under the ADA.

Defining Service Dog

The ADA also lays out the specifics of what makes a dog legally qualify as a service animal. Your dog must meet this definition for you to receive the rights and protections accorded to individuals with service dogs. To qualify:

✓ the dog must be individually trained to do work or perform tasks (at least one) for a person with a disability (you)

✓ the work or tasks must help mitigate your disability

The phrase "perform work or tasks" does not include providing comfort or emotional support simply by being at your side; the dog must actually do something for you that helps you with your disability. The dog must be trained to reliably perform this task as needed. Chapter 3: Is a Service Dog Right for You? gives lots of examples of the kinds of things your dog might be trained to do. The dog doesn't have to be professionally trained; it's perfectly acceptable for you to train it yourself.

There's some dispute among non-lawyers and lawyers alike regarding how many tasks a dog must know under this definition. In the text of the regulations, the word "tasks" is pluralized, so some people interpret that to mean "more than one." However, there are several ADA FAQs, which are specifically intended to clarify legal questions about the ADA, that use the singular form, "task," confirming that one is adequate. It also appears singular in other places in the ADA regulations. If you call the ADA hotline and ask, you may get different answers from different representatives - that's how cloudy this is. In practical terms this will almost certainly have no effect on you because virtually every service dog has multiple trained tasks so it will be a moot point. Those inclined to split legal hairs, however, might wish to be aware of this.

A service dog in training does not qualify as a service dog under the ADA. Although individual states may legislate access requirements for SDiTs, the ADA does not recognize them at all.

Public Access Rights

In addition to defining what makes a dog a service dog and who can have one, the big thing the ADA does is require businesses and nonprofit organizations that serve the public, as well as state and local governments, to allow your service dog to accompany you anywhere the general public is allowed to go. This includes grocery stores, restaurants, hospitals, movie theaters, hotels, and anywhere the general public is permitted. The ADA does require that the service dog must be "harnessed, leashed, or tethered" unless that would interfere with the dog's ability to work or the handler's disability prevents that.

A public entity can legally ask you and your service dog to leave the premises if:

- The service dog is out of control and you don't effectively control it

- The service dog isn't housebroken

- The entity is legally allowed to exclude service dogs under the special cases provisions of the ADA

The Two Questions

With guide dogs, it's obvious to most people what service the dog provides, but in the case of psychiatric service dogs, it's less apparent. To determine if a dog is a service dog, staff are permitted to ask two specific questions:

1) Is the dog a service animal required because of a disability?

2) What work or task has the dog been trained to perform?

You should be prepared to answer these questions. They are not permitted to ask you what your disability is, require special identification or medical information, or ask you to demonstrate your dog's work or task. If they do, you don't have to answer.

Although most businesses, especially larger ones, know these rules, you will run into people who don't. In such instances you can attempt to educate them, which might or might not be successful, or simply leave and follow up with a complaint or other response later. Chapter 9: Social Skills for Dogs and Handlers, delves into dealing with access challenges in greater detail.

While businesses are only permitted to ask you these two questions, random strangers face no such restrictions. They can and will ask you all kinds of things, such as what your disability is, and they aren't violating the ADA by doing so. You don't have to provide answers to such people, however, unless you choose to do so.

Just-in-case recordkeeping

Although businesses and other entities covered by the ADA can only ask you the two questions allowed by law, there are situations where documentation proving your status can be required. The biggest one is in a courtroom. If you end up in a lawsuit over discrimination against you and your use of your service dog, you'll have to prove that you're disabled and your dog meets the legal definition of service dog. This never happens to most handlers, but it's not out of the realm of possibility. Items you could produce to back up your case include:

- Medical records and letters from professionals who treat you for your disability or conditions related to it

- A Social Security disability letter of determination

- A video recording of your dog performing tasks or work

- Training logs, if your dog is owner-trained, or a statement from the service dog organization that trained your dog

- Evidence of any formal assessments your dog has passed, such as a public access test (PAT).

This sort of evidence could also be used to back up any deductions for service dog-related expenses that you claim on your federal tax return.

Exclusions and Special Cases

Service animals can be excluded from areas where their presence would "fundamentally alter the nature of the goods, services, or programs offered to the public," or where permitting them would violate safety requirements. For example, a service dog must be permitted in a hospital examining room or cafeteria but not in a burn unit or operating room where its presence would compromise the sterile environment. In general, it's a sterile area if the you and the staff have to wear special clothing. If you can just wear your street clothes, then generally your service dog would be permitted.

Zoos are another special case. Service dogs can be restricted from exhibits where the animals are natural predators or prey of dogs and might become agitated or aggressive, but the service dog team must be allowed access to all other areas.

Religious organizations or entities controlled by religious organizations are legally exempt from the ADA and don't have to permit service dogs, though many will if asked.

Per the ADA, allergies and fear of dogs are not valid reasons for denying access or refusing service to people with service dogs.

You do NOT need a prescription or letter from a medical professional documenting your disability to meet the disability requirement or to have a service dog. Some people choose to get one as documentation in the rare case they might face a court challenge, but it isn't required. You might need a letter for other purposes, such as to have your service dog in no-pets housing or to fly on commercial airlines in the cabin with you, but not for protection by the ADA.

In most situations, the ADA is the law that defines access rights for individuals with service animals, but legislation can be complex, and this is no exception. There are several more federal laws that are of interest to service dog handlers in particular situations.

Section 504 of the Rehabilitation Act of 1973

Somewhat oddly, federal agencies such as the U.S. Department of Veterans Affairs and the U.S. Department of Education don't have to comply with the ADA. There are laws that prevent them from discriminating against individuals with disabilities, however. The main one is Section 504 of The Rehabilitation Act of 1973 (The Rehab Act), a precursor to the ADA that is still in effect.

The Rehab Act covers government facilities, activities, and programs. Non-government entities that receive federal financial support, including private schools that receive federal funding, are also covered by this legislation. Multiple potential areas of discrimination, including discrimination in housing, education, employment, and transportation, are addressed. Each affected entity has its own set of 504 regulations that apply to it.

Taking a Service Dog to School

A student with a disability must be permitted to use a service animal. Which law guarantees this for you depends on whether the school you wish to attend is public or private and if it receives federal funds. In some cases, multiple laws apply.

The Individuals with Disabilities Education Act (IDEA) is the law of most interest to students in public school in kindergarten through twelfth grade who wish to be accompanied by a service dog in class. You might run across a variation of this acronym - IDEIA – in which case the extra I is for improvement. It resulted from a revision to the IDEA that occurred in 2004, but the original acronym is still used most often.

Public school classrooms are generally not considered public areas and are not covered by the ADA, but the IDEA can be of help. The IDEA requires public school systems to develop an Individualized Education Program (IEP) for each disabled child. A service animal can be added to a child's IEP and then it can accompany the child to class. Sometimes schools resist adding the service dog to the IEP and parents must go through an appeal process to make it happen.

Where the ADA applies, use of a service animal is a right that is not dependent on an IEP. Students with disabilities in public post-secondary education, such as college, are covered by the ADA (under Title II) and Section 504 of the Rehab Act rather than the IDEA. Private school students (both K-12 and post-secondary) that attend schools not operated by religious entities are covered by section III of the ADA and also have no need to turn to the IDEA for help. Schools can require documentation to verify that a student is disabled and requires the accommodation of being accompanied by a service dog.

Taking a Service Dog to Work

Title I of the ADA covers employment. The EEOC is in charge of creating and enforcing the regulations that implement it. These regulations don't require employers to automatically permit an individual with a disability to bring a service dog to work, but it does require them to consider it unless doing so would result in undue hardship. As a result, if you need your service dog at work, then you must ask for it. This is formally known as asking for a reasonable accommodation, although you don't have to use that specific phrase in your request.

A reasonable accommodation is a change to a job or work environment so that a qualified individual who has a disability can perform the essential functions of the job and access the "benefits and privileges of employment" that non-disabled employees do. That includes such things as employer-sponsored training, use of the company services such as a cafeteria or transportation, and access to social functions.

Your employer can ask you for documentation that shows you have an ADA-qualifying disability and the nature of the functional limitations that necessitate you having your service animal. According to the Job Accommodation Network (**www.askjan.org**), the employer can also ask you to provide evidence that your dog is trained and won't disrupt the workplace. This is where your training documentation or a statement from your trainer may come in to play.

The employer can offer you an alternative accommodation, but only if it would also be effective.

According to the EEOC, the definition of service animal provided by Title III of the ADA doesn't apply to Title I. Nor does Title I provide a definition of its own. This might seem unfortunate on the surface, but actually it's good news if your service dog is still in training because you can request a reasonable accommodation allowing your SDiT to accompany you even though it isn't a service dog yet. Of course, it would have to be far enough along in its training to ensure it wouldn't disrupt the workplace in any way.

Your employer may have no issue making an accommodation for you, but if you run into trouble, the Job Accommodation Network (JAN) is the go-to resource for help with job accommodations and disability employment issues. It's free, and you can contact them online (**www.askjan.org**) or by phone: (800)526-7234. TTY users call (877)781-9403. Your employer can make use of the same resource to help them reach an appropriate and legal decision.

State Service Dog Laws

Individual states cannot enact laws that override federal legislation such as the ADA, but they can augment it with their own rules. A number of states have done so, and a common amendment is to allow disabled individuals with service dogs in training the same access rights accorded to those with service dogs. This recognizes that to train a service dog for public access, it needs some practice! Another fairly frequent addition is to make it a misdemeanor to interfere with a service dog team or to misrepresent a pet as a service animal.

An increasing number of states have launched registration services for service dogs. Because the ADA states that there is no registration or certification required for service animals, the state cannot require you to register your service dog and these registries are voluntary. If you choose to register, you may receive a tag for your dog's collar or some other form of identification.

Such state provisions can change without much warning, but there's a great place for keeping an eye on them: the Animal Legal & Historical Center website operated by Michigan State University College of Law (**www.animallaw.info**). There you will find a bunch of great resources including a table of all 50 states' assistance animal laws (**https://www.animallaw.info/topic/table-state-assistance-animal-laws**).

Obtaining a Housing Accommodation

What can you do if you live in "no pets" housing and you need a service dog? An apartment or rental home is not a place that's open to the public and access rights aren't covered by the ADA. This is where the Fair Housing Act (FHAct), or in some cases another part of Section 504, comes in. Both of these require housing providers to provide "reasonable accommodations" to individuals with disabilities. Reasonable accommodations include permitting assistance animals and emotional support animals "in all areas of the premises where persons are allowed to go, unless doing so would impose an undue financial and administrative burden or would fundamentally alter the nature of the housing provider's services."

Key points of these provisions include that:

✓ **The definition of assistance animals is broader than the legal definition for service animals.** It includes animals which provide emotional support only, without being individually trained to do so, as long as you have a disability-related need for such support. That essentially means your SDiT or even prospect would both qualify.

✓ **Breed, size, and weight limitations may not be applied to an assistance animal.** Note that under the FHAct other animals besides dogs can be assistance animals.

✓ **Housing providers can ask you to provide documentation of your disability and your related need for an assistance animal if your disability isn't apparent.** This happens often to people with mental health disabilities. The documentation request can be satisfied by a letter from a physician, psychiatrist, social worker, or other mental health professional. The letter must state that you have a disability and that the animal will provide disability-related assistance or emotional support. You cannot be required to provide access to your medical records or medical providers or to provide extensive, detailed documentation. Figure 6-1 provides a sample letter you can adapt to your needs. Additional sample letters are included in the appendix.

✓ **A pet deposit cannot be required.** Conditions applied to pets, such as requiring a pet deposit, cannot be applied to assistance animals. If your dog damages the property though, you can be required to pay for repairs.

Figure 7-1 demonstrates what a letter requesting a housing accommodation might look like.

Figure 7-1: Sample Medical Provider Letter Requesting Service Dog Housing Accommodation

---

(print on letterhead)

To Whom It May Concern:

[Your full name] is my patient and is under my care. **[He/She]** meets the definition for disability under the Americans with Disabilities Act, the Fair Housing Act, and the Rehabilitation Act of 1973.

[His/Her] disability causes certain functional limitations. These limitations include [list major life activities that are impacted].

In order to help alleviate these difficulties, and to enhance his/her ability to live independently and to fully use and enjoy the dwelling unit you own and/or administer, **[he/she]** requires the assistance of **[his/her]** service dog. The presence of this assistance animal is necessary for **[his/her]** health because it is individually trained to perform tasks that help mitigate **[his/her]** disability.

Thank you for providing this reasonable accommodation for my patient.

Sincerely,

Signature: _____ Date: _____

Your request for a reasonable accommodation can be denied if:

1) The assistance animal poses a direct threat to the health and safety of others that cannot be reduced or eliminated by another reasonable accommodation.

   or

2) The assistance animal would cause substantial physical damage to the property of others that cannot be reduced or eliminated by another reasonable accommodation.

or

3) Granting the accommodation would impose an undue financial and administrative burden or would fundamentally alter the nature of the housing provider's services.

Number three might sound like an easy out for the housing provider, but it's not. There are very few things that would fall under that heading. One of these that has been reported is that if your dog is of a breed that is considered dangerous by the housing provider's insurance provider and its presence would drastically jack up the cost of the provider's insurance, that increased cost could potentially fall under number three and cause your request for an accommodation to be legally denied.

State and local government facilities and programs and public accommodations such as universities are covered by the ADA. In these places, service dogs must be allowed. Such places can only ask you the two questions allowed under the ADA (see above) and can't require special documentation such as a letter from a medical professional. All other ADA regulations apply to them as well. Table 7-2 helps clarify which law applies to different kinds of housing. In some cases, multiple laws may apply.

Although most housing is covered by the FHAct or another of these laws, there are situations where none of them apply. The exceptions listed under the Fair Housing Act in table 7-1 offer several examples, including single-family housing rented without the use of a broker. There isn't any legal requirement that service dogs be permitted in such settings.

Table 7-2: Housing Laws That Affect Service Dogs

Statue	*Housing Covered*
Fair Housing Act	Applies to most housing for sale or rent. Exceptions include (a) buildings with four or fewer units where the landlord lives in one of them, and (b) private owners of three or fewer single family houses who don't use real estate brokers or agents.
Section 504 of The Rehabilitation Act of 1973	Applies to programs that receive federal assistance such as public or subsidized housing (but not Section 8 housing).
Americans with Disabilities Act	Applies to state and local government facilities and programs such as the public housing authority and public accommodations such as universities.

Flying with a Service Dog or SDiT

Airports are covered by the ADA, but assistance animals on airplanes come under the Air Carrier Access Act (ACAA). This law permits service animals and emotional support animals to travel in an airplane cabin of commercial airlines with their disabled owner. The airline cannot charge any additional fees for this.

While some people with service dogs, such as a blind person with a service dog, can just show up at the gate and board, individuals with psychiatric disabilities usually have to jump through an extra hoop. You must notify the airline 48 hours ahead of your flight and provide documentation showing your status as a service team. A letter dated within a year from a medical professional will satisfy the documentation requirement but it must include that:

✓ You have a mental or emotional disability that is listed in the Diagnostic and Statistical Manual of Mental Disorders (DSM-IV).

✓ You need the service animal or emotional support animal as an accommodation for air travel and/or at your destination

✓ The person providing the letter is a licensed mental health professional and you are under their care

✓ The date issued, number, and jurisdiction of the letter writer's license

The letter doesn't have to state your specific diagnosis, but it must mention that your disability is included in the DSM-IV. Sharp-eyed readers may note that the DSM-IV has been replaced by the DSM-V in practical use; however, the wording of the law hasn't been updated yet. Realistically it's unlikely an airline would notice or complain if a letter references the DSM-V instead. Figure 7-2 provides an example (print on letterhead).

Figure 7-2: Sample Letter for Flying with a Psychiatric Service Animal

---

(print on letterhead)

To Whom It May Concern:

I am currently treating **[full name]** for a mental health or emotional disability recognized in the Diagnostic and Statistical Manual of Mental Disorders (DSM-IV). This person needs **[his/her]** dog to travel as a **[psychiatric service animal or emotional support animal]** for air travel and/or for activity at the destination. My **[type of license]** was issued in the state or jurisdiction of **[location]** in **[year]**.

Sincerely,

Signature: _____ Date: _____

Some service dog handlers keep a generic letter similar to this on hand because it can be used in several situations including for flying and for requesting an accommodation in no pets housing. Typically the letter must be less than a year old to be accepted. No, it's not fair that people with psychiatric disabilities are treated differently than people with other disabilities, but that's the way the law currently is.

If your service dog is still in training, you most likely can take advantage of the inclusion of emotional support animals (ESAs) under this law. The ACAA doesn't cover SDiTs. Some airlines will accept SDiTs, but if not, you can go the ESA route. The rules for emotional support animals are the same as for service dogs - you still must have a disability and provide a letter from a medical professional as described above, but the animal doesn't have to be trained; simply providing companionship qualifies. Appendix B includes a sample letter for flying accompanied by an ESA.

You can find information regarding where, when, and to whom to submit your documentation by visiting the airline's website or asking the agent when you make your reservation.

Reporting a Violation of Your Rights

Just because you have a legal right to do something with your service dog or SDiT doesn't mean everyone you encounter will know and abide by that. Sometimes you may just need to educate them. If that doesn't work, you can opt to file a report to the appropriate federal authority. Before taking that step, it's advisable to investigate any grievance procedures the offending entity has in place. You may get quicker and more effective action through that avenue rather than jumping straight into filing a complaint with the feds. In cases where you don't get satisfaction, you can always escalate later. Table 7-3 lists where to report violations of the federal laws discussed in this chapter.

Table 7-3: Reporting Violations

Statute	How to Report
Americans with Disabilities Act, Title II and Title III	Complaints can be filed by mail or online. U.S. Department of Justice 950 Pennsylvania Avenue, N.W. Civil Rights Division Disability Rights Section 1425 NYAV Washington, DC 20530 **http://www.ada.gov** 800-514-0301 (voice) 800-514-0383 (TTY)
Section 504 of The Rehabilitation Act of 1973	Complaints must be filed with the federal agency that funds the entity.
Fair Housing Act	Complaints should be filed with the Department of Housing and Urban Development (HUD) Office of Fair Housing and Equal Opportunity. You can file them through the HUD website or by phone. **http://www.hud.gov/fairhousing** 800-669-9777 (voice) 800-927-9275 (TTY)
Air Carrier Access Act (ACAA)	File complaints via web (preferred) or mail. Aviation Consumer Protection Division Attn: C-75-D U.S. Department of Transportation 1200 New Jersey Ave, SE Washington, D.C. 20590 **https://www.transportation.gov/airconsumer/file-consumer-complaint** The U.S. Department of Transportation maintains a toll-free hotline (800-778-4838) but it's for obtaining real-time help with a problem, not for reporting violations.
IDEA	Under the IDEA, each state is required to develop and implement complaint procedures that adhere to IDEA requirements. To resolve a dispute, you must go through your state's educational agency (SEA) (for example, the Department of Public Instruction) rather than through a federal agency. You can usually find the procedures on the web by entering *your_state_name + idea + complaint* into any major search engine.

Tax Breaks for Service Dog Expenses

With adoption fees, vet bills, training costs and more, the costs of acquiring and owning a service dog can quickly mount up. The good news is that medical expenses, including those related to a service animal, can potentially be taken as deductions on your federal tax return. However, this will only have an effect on your bottom line if:

- ✓ your total medical and dental expenses exceed 10% of your adjusted gross income (AGI). Only the amount that exceeds 10% is deductible (unless you or your spouse was born before January 2, 1949, then it's 7.5%).

- ✓ you have enough itemized deductions so that the total exceeds your standard deduction and is therefore worth taking.

IRS Publication 502, which details allowable medical and dental expenses, says:

"You can include in medical expenses the costs of buying, training, and maintaining a guide dog or other service animal to assist a visually impaired or hearing disabled person, or a person with other physical disabilities. In general, this includes any costs, such as food, grooming, and veterinary care, incurred in maintaining the health and vitality of the service animal so that it may perform its duties."

The text of Publication 502 does say "physical disabilities," so you might think that a service animal for a psychiatric or mental disability isn't covered, but further guidance put out by the IRS specifically addresses the deductibility of expenses related to service animals who assist individuals with mental health disabilities. IRS Informational Letter 2010-0129 states:

"The costs of buying, training, and maintaining a service animal to assist an individual with mental disabilities may qualify as medical care if the taxpayer can establish that the taxpayer is using the service animal primarily for medical care to alleviate a mental defect or illness and that the taxpayer would not have paid the expenses but for the disease or illness."

To claim these deductions you must be able to back up your position that you would not have had the expenses if you didn't have the mental illness. Credible evidence might include whether a physician diagnosed your condition and recommended a service dog, along with proof that your dog is trained to assist you, or other evidence that shows your dog qualifies as a service dog under the ADA. You'll also need to save receipts and other documents that verify your exact expenses, just as for other deductions.

This information was carefully researched, but please don't take it as official, legal tax advice. Decisions about what to deduct on your tax return are best made in consultation with a tax advisor or accountant. This information is simply intended to help.

Chapter 8

Getting to Know the Service Dog Community

In this chapter

➢ Meeting and learning from other handlers online

➢ Becoming familiar with major service dog organizations

➢ Finding trustworthy answers to legal questions

Whether you're considering your first service dog, have one already, or are just curious about them, you are not alone. As the concept of service dogs for disabilities beyond blindness has come into wider acceptance, a lot of people want to discuss possibilities and exchange experiences. There may be few to zero service dog handlers in your neighborhood, but there are many, many of them online. Even if you don't have Internet access at home, you can always get it at your local public library. The online community includes:

✓ forums for service dog handlers to exchange ideas and information

✓ websites of organizations that support and promote the use of service dogs

✓ resources for help with legal questions related to use of an assistance animal

This chapter highlights the best and most helpful of these, plus a few that may be a little less helpful but that you should know about anyway. There's no need to go on a web binge and plow your way through every one of these in one sitting; instead pick one or two resources at a time and get to know each well. Dip a toe in here and there until you find what you need.

Service Dogs on Social Media

Facebook, YouTube, Instagram and other social media sites provide a handy way to meet and get to know other members of the service dog community. They can also be an excellent source of training examples and advice, as long as you are discerning about which advice you choose to follow. There's plenty of junk advice mixed in with the good stuff, but as soon as you build up your knowledge about psychiatric service dogs a bit, you'll quickly be able to recognize misinformation and filter it out while still benefitting from the generous sharing performed by many members of the service dog community.

Joining Facebook Groups

There are numerous groups on Facebook (**www.facebook.com**) dedicated to service dogs. You can find groups that cover all types of service dogs, psychiatric service dogs specifically, or that serve as a meeting point for handlers in a particular geographic area. Some are busy and packed with frequent posts, while others provide a more intimate environment. All of them require you to join the group in order to view any of the posts. For the most part they are very open to accepting new members and your request should receive a response the day you submit it or within a couple of days at most.

The plentiful supply of Facebook groups can be overwhelming, and if you run out and join all of them you'll get buried in a stream of new posts which will include a lot of redundant information. It's better to try a couple at a time until you find a few favorites. Here's a starting list, but you can find many more using Facebook search:

- ✓ **Service Dogs for Invisible Disabilities** (>12, 685 members) - This is the largest Facebook group focused on service dogs. People here often have both physical and psychiatric disabilities. The Files section includes information on getting started for new handlers along with other useful information.

✓ **Psychiatric Service Dogs** (>3,229 members) - As the name implies, this group focuses specifically on issues related to the use of service dogs for assistance with mental health disabilities.

✓ **Service Dog Organization and Trainer Reviews** (>1,800 members) - Unlike the other Facebook groups, this one isn't for open discussion. Posts are limited to questions about specific training programs and help finding a program or trainer. The Files section contains reviews of programs by people who have used them.

✓ **Service Dog Gearaholics** (>500 members) - Q & A about service dog gear, including patches, vests, harnesses, booties, or just about anything else. Items can be bought and sold here, unlike most other Facebook service dog forums.

Before you even consider posting to any of these groups, take the time to read the group rules and familiarize yourself with the type and flavor of posts it contains. The rules may be listed in the group description, a pinned post at the top of the forum, or in a file under the Files tab. The Files tab is a good place to look for other things too. You may find FAQs, the text of particular laws you're interested in, and other goodies such as the text of Walmart's policy regarding service animals.

It's best to lurk and learn before posting. In a paradoxical situation, people come to these groups for help and advice, and after innocently asking a poorly worded question or posting a picture that's considered inappropriate, get verbally piled on as everyone rushes to correct them. It seems to happen because forum members are very protective of proper service dog etiquette as well as very concerned that people correctly understand laws related to service dog teams. If you violate those tenets, other forum members will let you know, and not always nicely, and who wants to start off a relationship like that? You can avoid this pitfall and get the best use of forums by following the local customs, as defined in the forum's rules.

Examples of rules you'll encounter include:

- ✓ No advertising or soliciting allowed.

- ✓ Place TRIGGER WARNING at the top of any post about something that may be upsetting to people who are sensitive to that subject.

- ✓ Don't add comments to threads marked CLOSED even though Facebook will let you.

Some groups allow you to freely mention program and product names but others restrict it in an effort to avoid spamming, advertisements, and other issues. Know what the forum you're about to post in allows before you hit Enter.

Every forum has one or many administrators. If you're unsure of the rules, ask them via private message (PM) before posting.

Learning by Example on YouTube

If you'd like to see some examples of service dogs in action, YouTube (**www.youtube.com**) has a decent supply of video clips demonstrating service dog tasks. These are posted by individuals who are owner-training, service dog trainers, and people who have service dogs and just want to educate the public. The video clips vary greatly in quality, but if you find some that are right on target for your needs, chances are the person who posted them has an entire collection online that you can view.

As with other online resources, YouTube is a bit of a free-for-all, so the items you find here haven't been run through any vetting process to confirm authenticity or accuracy; once you've been studying service dogs for just little while though, you'll be able to tell which ones offer credible information. Just Google "YouTube service dog" to get started. You can also look for a particular task by using a more specific search, such as "YouTube service dog blocking."

Following Service Dog Teams on Instagram

You won't find much practical help on Instagram (**www.instagram.com**), but if you'd like to see lots of pictures of psychiatric service dogs and their handlers, you'll find plenty here. This site also includes video clips. They tend to be shorter than those on YouTube, but they show a larger variety of dog breeds in action. Some handlers create an Instagram page for their dog as a way of tracking and demonstrating that it does, in fact, have service dog training. They may also use these pages as material to show people when conducting a fundraising campaign to help cover training costs.

Benefitting from Bloggers

Wouldn't it be nice if you could peek in on the lives of other service dog handlers or learn from service dog trainers around the country? Through blogs, you can! Blog is a shortened word for web log. A blog is an online chronicle, often written in a diary-like format, detailing information and experiences over time. Blogging software allows writers to format and organize their posts with minimal need for technical know-how, which means pretty much anyone can do it. Both individuals and organizations write blogs to help get their stories out, and you can be one of the beneficiaries. You might even want to start a blog of your own service dog experience somewhere down the road.

WordPress (**www.wordpress.com**) and Blogger (**www.blogger.com**) are the most widely-used blogging platforms. Neither of these offers particularly good search capabilities so you're better off using Google to find service dog blogs. If you visit WordPress.com, you can search billions of WordPress posts through a search form, but that search will bring up a lot of extra stuff you're probably not interested in. This is because many WordPress blogs are hosted on WordPress.com but many more are reside elsewhere. That's true of Blogger blogs as well; many take advantage of free hosting at blogspot.com but they can be hosted anywhere. If you try to go directly to blogspot.com, you may get a little confused, because you will be automatically redirected to the domain blogger.com and offered the opportunity to start your own blog instead of finding blogs to read.

So how can you dip into this bounty most easily? Google search is the answer. To find blog articles on topics ranging from general to specific simply tailor your search terms to your needs. For example, you might search for "psychiatric service dog blog" or "service dog blog medication retrieval" or "service dog deep pressure therapy." Keep in mind that the majority of these blogs are written by private individuals. While they are packed with interesting and useful information, a significant number will also contain inaccurate or downright bad advice, so to state the obvious, don't believe everything you read! You'll be able to sort fact from fiction pretty quickly once you've read this book, so don't hesitate to dive into the fascinating world of blogs.

Service Dog Organizations

The following organizations are dedicated to serving the needs of people partnered with service dogs. They are masters of providing information and advocacy and have done so very successfully for years, providing incalculable benefits to service dog handlers. None of them provide or train service dogs, but they do offer plenty of guidance on the process. They don't always see eye-to-eye on every topic, so it's helpful to know where each one stands.

Psychiatric Service Dog Partners (PSDP) (www.psychdogpartners.org)

It's hard to say enough good things about this organization. Based in Rock Hill, South Carolina, PSDP is a successor organization to a previous advocacy group called the Psychiatric Service Dog Society (PSDS). It was formed in 2012 and achieved 501(c)(3) charitable organization status in 2015. Since inception, PSDP has worked to fulfill its mission: "to promote the mental health of people using service dogs for psychiatric disabilities by educating, advocating, providing expertise, facilitating peer support, and promoting responsible service dog training and handling."

This organization actively advocates for the rights of service dog handlers by tracking proposed legislation, filing legal briefs, and providing recognized expertise through presentations and media appearances. They even host an annual Psychiatric Service Dog Convention. Be sure to visit their website, where you'll find a wealth of information about many aspects of obtaining and using a psychiatric service dog, along with practical resources such as printable flyers containing service dog information.

International Association of Assistance Dog Partners (IAADP) (www.iaadp.org)

IAADP is a nonprofit membership organization created in 1993 to serve the needs of individuals partnered with a service dog of any type, whether for physical or psychiatric disabilities. Its mission is to:

1) Provide assistance dog partners with a voice in the assistance dog field;

2) Enable those partnered with guide dogs, hearing dogs and service dogs to work together on issues of mutual concern;

3) Foster the disabled person / assistance dog partnership.

Membership is primarily geared toward people partnered with a service dog, but service dog trainers and other people interested in service dogs can also join.

IAADP is perhaps best known among service dog handlers for its IAADP Minimum Training Standards for Public Access. The training standards provide an itemized list of the recommended amount of training, obedience standards, and specific manners a service dog should have for working in public. While this doesn't rise to the level of a legally recognized standard, it's commonly used by service dog trainers to set goals and to help assess a dog's readiness for working in public. The list is available for free on the IAADP website.

This organization is going through a transition due to the passing of a co-founder and driving force, Joan Froling. Even though it's currently less active than it used to be, it is still a valuable resource and advocate for service dog teams.

Assistance Dogs International (ADI)
(www.assistancedogsinternational.org)

ADI is an industry membership organization for nonprofit assistance dog organizations around the world. Service dog providers can apply for accreditation by ADI and be included in their online directory of assistance dog programs, which is currently the most extensive such directory available online. Although ADI doesn't serve handlers directly, their activities impact the handler community.

The concept of setting standards for organizations which provide service dogs is admirable, but this organization is not without controversy. For example, its member training organizations must provide IDs to service dog teams, and IDs are fraught with controversy in the service dog community because the ADA specifically states that IDs are not required, but gatekeepers still sometimes ask for them because they don't know the law. Encouraging the use of IDs is considered by many to be against the best interests of disabled individuals. ADI encourages the adoption of laws that require IDs and also require a service dog to wear an identifying harness, vest, or backpack, which is also contrary to the ADA. They also publish and promote their ADI Minimum Standards & Ethics, which among other things require service dogs to know at least three tasks rather than at least one (task or work) as required by the ADA.

Despite what seems to be a desire to be the arbiter of standards (standards for trainers, for handlers, for dogs....), they do offer resources of value to the service dog handler community. One of these is a model public access test, which was designed to be administered by ADI member trainers but is published on their website for anyone's use. Even if you don't agree with their standards push, or perhaps especially then, this is an organization you should be familiar with.

Service Dog Central (www.servicedogcentral.org)

While it's not technically an organization, Service Dog Central is a fantastic resource center and gathering place for members of the service dog community. It's a busy, constantly updated site that includes a community message board where you can ask questions and read about other people's experiences. Visit it to find additional information on service dog training and handling, access issues, handler rights, and legal issues.

Resources for Answering Legal Questions

For both new and experienced service dog handlers, legal issues can be some of the trickiest territory to navigate. How do you know the advice you are given is accurate? Where can you refer "the other side of the argument" so they fully understand their legal obligations? The following organizations are recognized and reliable expert sources for both of these purposes.

Job Accommodation Network (JAN) (www.askjan.ORG)

If you or your employer have questions about service dogs in the workplace, the answer can most likely be found on the JAN website. If not, you are welcome to call them or contact them online. JAN is a free service provided by the U.S. Department of Labor's Office of Disability Employment Policy (ODEP). Resources available on this site include:

- *Employees' Practical Guide to Negotiating and Requesting Reasonable Accommodations Under the Americans with Disabilities Act (ADA):* Provides advice on how to request an accommodation and negotiate with your employer so you can get what you need.

- *Employers' Practical Guide to Reasonable Accommodation Under the Americans with Disabilities Act (ADA) :* Guides employers on how to handle accommodation requests and gives specific examples of reasonable accommodations for different disabilities.

- **Accommodation Information by Disability: A to Z:** This section of the site contains accommodation ideas organized by type of disability. You may find useful ideas here, beyond service dog use, of accommodations that could help you work despite your disability.

This isn't an online-only resource. You (or your employer) can call JAN to discuss your personal situation at (800)526-7234 (Voice) (877)781-9403 (TTY).

Animal Legal & Historical Center (www.animallaw.info)

This site, which is published and maintained by the Michigan State University College of Law, collects, organizes, and explains laws and legal challenges pertaining to animal law. One of its key resources is the *Table of State Assistance Animal Laws*, which is a complete, state-by-state listing of laws that pertain to service animals. If you're planning a road trip and want to know the laws of states you'll pass through, you can find them here. The table identifies associated statues and includes links to the official text.

ADA Information Line

Information and technical assistance about the Americans with Disabilities Act (ADA) is available through the ADA Information Line at 800-514-0301 (Voice). TTY users call 800-514-0383. You can also use this number to request ADA publications via mail. If you call on a weekend you probably won't get a person but can still use the automated system to obtain information.

Chapter 9

Social Skills for Dogs & Handlers

In this chapter

- ➤ Learning about service dog etiquette
- ➤ How to properly socialize your dog
- ➤ Dealing with drive-by petting and nosey people
- ➤ Coping with an access challenge without melting down
- ➤ Opting in to service dog advocacy
- ➤ Having a little fun with social annoyances

Potential service dog handlers always underestimate the amount of attention and interaction a service dog draws. Whether you're in the grocery store, a movie theatre, or on the bus, chances are someone (or multiple people) are going to come up to you and start asking questions. The vast majority of the time it's simply the result of unbounded human curiosity coupled with obliviousness to the possibility you might not want to share your personal information and just want to complete your errands unmolested. In much rarer cases, it will be business gatekeepers questioning if your dog is really a service dog, which they are entitled to do as long as they follow legal guidelines regarding how they go about it.

Some of the questions you can expect:

- Can I pet your dog (regardless of whether your dog is wearing a Working, Do NOT Pet patch)?

- Why do you need a service dog (i.e. you don't look disabled)?

- Is that really a service dog?

- Who are you training the dog for?

- It must be so hard for you when you will have to give that dog up (i.e. back to a training organization), I couldn't do it…

- Where can I get a service dog vest for my dog?

You can't completely prevent such encounters, but you can reduce their frequency. You can also reduce the amount of stress such personal prying might cause you by preparing yourself for the most common situations with a plan of action.

It's also important to recognize your ethical responsibilities as a service dog handler. You should be well-versed in service dog etiquette and know what to do if someone tries to deny you access to a place you know perfectly well you and your dog are allowed to go.

Make sure you know which law applies when so you don't incorrectly accuse someone of violating your rights or claim they're violating a law that doesn't even apply to that situation. For example, threatening to file an ADA violation complaint with the U.S. Department of Justice because you were denied access with your SDiT would be a mistake because SDiTs aren't covered by the ADA, only service dogs are. Some states have laws that cover SDiTs, so it might be a violation of state law, but it isn't a violation of the ADA. Chapter 7: Knowing Service Dog Laws, will help ensure you have accurate information at hand.

Practicing Service Dog Etiquette

The ADA states that your service animal must be under your control and can't potty indoors, but that's about it. Even though it's not written into any law, the majority of service dog handlers strive to far exceed those minimum requirements. The ability to be accompanied by your service dog in places that are usually off limits to dogs comes from legal rights accorded to you as a person with a disability. There are moral responsibilities that come with those legal privileges even though they aren't codified in any law.

Your goal should be to avoid disrupting the normal flow of operations so your service dog can assist you without inconveniencing anyone else. That's not always possible, but often it is. "I didn't even know a dog was in here!" is the ultimate compliment for many handlers.

✓ Staying out of the way - Teach your dog to "go under" and/or tuck out of the way. Small and medium-sized dogs can fit completely beneath a waiting room chair and become virtually invisible. Larger dogs that cannot fit can lie between your legs and the chair. In restaurants, opt for a booth over a table. Send your dog underneath and nobody will even know it's present. Nobody should have to step over your dog.

✓ Keep your dog exceptionally groomed - If your dog tends to shed, and unless it's a Mexican hairless that's very likely so, then give it a brush to remove loose fur before you head out. If it needs a bath, bathe it. Keep any drool under control.

✓ If it's raining, stuff a washcloth or dishtowel in your pocket and dry your pup's feet when you enter a building. It could save somebody from slipping and falling courtesy of wet paw prints.

✓ Be cognizant of other people's needs - Legally, fear of dogs or allergies aren't valid reasons to deny you access, but they are still very legitimate problems for some people. Some people aren't comfortable around dogs due to religious beliefs. If you end up beside someone with any of these issues, give them some extra space even if it delays you a bit.

✓ Keep your dog leashed when in public settings. Local leash laws apply to service dogs. An exception can be made when service dog must be off leash to perform a task.

✓ A service dog should remain on the floor (preferable) or be carried. Service dogs shouldn't ride in shopping carts or sit on restaurant seating.

✓ Don't allow your dog to initiate contact with other people while working. This takes more training for some dogs than others. Their focus should strictly be on you.

✓ If your dog does accidentally make a mess or cause damage, clean it up!

✓ At all times, keep the safety of your dog in mind. Don't work a dog that needs down time due to injury or illness or a female in heat.

Socializing Your Dog

When you're out and about, you're going to run into people and situations that look startlingly different to your dog. Ideally your PSD will be unflappable, but it can take a while to get to that state. Actively preparing for such encounters is called socialization, and how you go about it may be different than you'd expect. Especially while your dog is still undergoing initial training, some of your outings will have the primary purpose of working on socialization skills.

The number one mistake newbies to dog training make when attempting to socialize their dog is very basic - they misunderstand exactly what it is they're supposed to be doing. Most understand that socialization means exposing your pup to new things so they're prepared when they encounter them "in the wild," but going about it the wrong way can backfire, and you can end up with a dog that's reactive to the very thing you were trying to desensitize him to! Always remember, socializing does **not** mean flooding your dog with a new experience and repeating until they stop reacting negatively to it. Forcing your dog into new situations can easily backfire and result in a reactive dog, either immediately or, if the dog is a puppy, when they get a bit older (at which point you'll be wondering why he's suddenly terrified of people with hats!).

Proper socialization provides a positive experience. The dog is introduced to new things, such as a child with a scary bulging backpack, in a way that allows the dog to come out of the encounter feeling successful. Try to make it a positive experience rather than just an experience. It's okay if the dog is a bit nervous in the beginning, but the key is not to force the situation. Allow the dog to escape from the situation if it wants to leave, but you can encourage the dog to return. If it won't, the challenge is probably too hard at the moment. Try to make it easier or return to it later.

Using the backpack example, if you've come up on a child wearing a backpack and your dog is afraid and isn't quickly getting over it, let it go and move away. Later you can put a bulky backpack on a person your dog knows and loves and try again. That favorite person will also know how to play your dog's favorite game. Once your dog is confident with that, you can consider approaching an unknown stranger again.

Your service dog does not have to love everyone and be the social star of the dog park to be a successful service dog. Dogs have different personalities, just like people. Some are outgoing and love anyone who might provide a few pats on the head. Others prefer to get to know someone a bit first, before being handled by them. Either personality can make a good PSD. In fact, the more reserved dog might do a little better as it will be less likely to be distracted by strangers making kissy noises at it (yes that happens). Your goal should be for your dog to behave calmly and follow your commands even when other people or dogs are around. It's *normal* for mature dogs to have no desire to play with a bunch of unfamiliar dogs at a dog park. Puppies play together more easily, but adult dogs in groups, not so much, and that's okay, so don't worry about it.

The goal of socialization is to teach your dog that the world is full of new, interesting, and sometimes strange people and things, but that they aren't scary or dangerous, and for the dog to trust your lead when encountering new things. Your dog should feel confident that you can be counted on to keep it safe and will only ask it to do things it's safe to do. Don't worry about introducing your SDiT to every possible thing it might experience, such as every surface you might walk on. If you've introduced a variety of surfaces, then when you encounter a new one, approach it confidently and your dog will follow your lead, having done so many times before.

Deflecting Unwanted Interest

If you're an extrovert who takes pleasure in interacting with people wherever you go and don't mind answering personal questions about yourself and your dog, you can skip this section. For a lot of PSD handlers, however, such questions feel like an intrusion on personal privacy that they'd be pleased to do without. If you fall into the latter group, you'll be happy to hear that there are ways you can escape revealing your entire personal history to a stranger every time you go to the grocery store.

Top strategies include:

- ✓ Leverage body language to broadcast a do not disturb message.

- ✓ Prepare yourself with automatic answers to the most common questions.

- ✓ Arm yourself with information cards.

- ✓ Keep your dog's appearance neat and professional.

- ✓ Teach your dog commands to use during unwanted encounters.

Until you start going around in public with your service dog, these tactics might seem like overkill to you. This chapter will be waiting right here after you take your first outings and find out just how much of an attention magnet a service dog really is. If you don't enjoy being the star attraction (even if that's true on some days but not others), try out these techniques. At the very least they will reduce and ease awkward moments, and they may just become indispensable tools.

Putting Body Language to Work

At first, deliberately sending off "don't talk to me" vibes might feel like you're being a bit rude, but the easiest way out of an uncomfortable encounter is to avoid the conversation in the first place. Most people will read your body language correctly and leave you alone. If you're shy and/or introverted you may already be a master of this, but for those who are not, these tips will help. Make use of the ones you feel most comfortable with and pass on the rest.

- ✓ Keep your gaze straight ahead, focused on where you're going, and try not to meet other people's glances. Many will take a friendly smile as an invitation to pump you for information about your dog, so don't give them one. This doesn't mean you have to go around with a look of death on your face, a neutral expression will suffice.

- ✓ Consider wearing headphones or earbuds, even if you're not actually listening to music.

- ✓ If someone speaks to you (other than a gatekeeper legitimately asking you a question), pretend you didn't hear them. For example, turn and speak to a companion or to your dog.

- ✓ Consider putting a prong collar on your dog. It doesn't even need to be attached to the leash; its mere presence will reduce drive-by petting and similar encounters. People seem to take it as a signal the dog isn't friendly. (If the collar is attached to the leash, make sure it fits properly and you know the correct way to use it.)

Even if you send out "do not disturb" signals, and especially if you opt not to go that route, people are going to initiate conversations with you and talk to your dog. "Hi puppy puppy! You are such a cutie-wootie!" for example. This is much easier to endure if you have a strategy ready to whip out.

Practicing Speaking (Really)

Strategy #1: Practice. This might sound a little hokie at first, but it will help immensely. Enlist a friend to play gatekeeper or nosey person in the checkout line and practice responding to their questions until your answers flow smoothly.

Every handler should know what they will say if asked the two questions gatekeepers are allowed to ask:

1) Is that a service animal required because of a disability?

2) What work or task has the dog been trained to perform?

The answer to number one is easy- just say yes. If your dog is still an SDiT and your state is one that permits access for SDiTs, you can say that it's a service dog in training and service dogs in training are allowed access under state law.

Number two is the one handlers stumble over most often, especially PSD handlers. You know you're legit so why is answering this so stressful? Who knows, but for some people, it causes an instant sweat and your tongue suddenly forgets how to form words. You can avoid that, however, by having a stock response ready. Some handlers go with "medical alert" or "medical response" or the wordier but slightly more informative:

✓ medical alert - she warns me if I'm about to become ill

or

✓ medical response - he helps me if I become ill.

Some handlers choose to be more specific: He interrupts panic attacks. She alerts me to changes in my mental state. He picks up things for me because my medicine makes me dizzy. She leads me to a safe place in an emergency. He summons help if I need it. You don't have to reveal personal medical details though unless you choose to do so.

Find a willing friend or fellow service dog handler and practice your answers to the two questions. Work on your answers to the other questions listed above as well. A little role playing can go a long way here. There is no right answer to such questions. The right answer is the one you feel comfortable giving. Some handlers simply state "I don't feel comfortable sharing my personal medical information." Or you might opt to enter into friendly conversation or to educate. "You can get vests online but it would be illegal for you to pretend your pet is a service dog so that would be a very bad idea."

Whether or not you let someone pet your service dog is totally up to you. People will ask you, even when your dog has "DO NOT PET" in capital letters on his back, so be prepared. You might say "no, not when he's working" or you might feel it's okay and give permission.

Handing Out Information Cards

Strategy #2: If you'd like a polite but firm way to escape the question hailstorm, consider investing in some inexpensive business cards, which you can get from cheaply from VistaPrint (**vistaprint.com**) or your favorite source. Design your own or copy the one shown in Figure 9-1. Carry them in your wallet or in a pocket in your dog's working vest. When someone questions you, simply say "Here's a card that explains all that," and hand one over.

By design, the card shown in Figure 9-1 is generic and doesn't contain personal information. The front has information for the curious and the back provides details for gatekeepers on the two questions they may ask, plus the phone number for the ADA Info Line. Some handlers like cards that get more personal. Such cards often include a picture of the dog and describe its specific tasks, but give careful thought to how much personal detail you wish to pass out to strangers via your cards.

Figure 9-1: Service Dog Information Card (front and back)

Service Dog Information (Yes I'm cute, please ignore me!)

A service dog is individually trained to help a person with a disability. Not all disabilities are visible.

For example, a person with PTSD may have a dog trained to interrupt panic attacks. A person with diabetes may have a dog trained to alert to changes in blood sugar.

Service dogs come in all shapes and sizes!

When you see a service dog...

- Don't pet or distract the dog. In fact it's best to ignore them completely!

- Don't ask about the nature of the person's disability. That's personal, private information.

Service Dog Access: Protected By Federal Law

In accordance with the Americans with Disabilities Act of 1990 (ADA), a service dog must be permitted to accompany its handler in places that provide goods or services to the public.

Businesses May Ask:
1. Is this a service dog required because of a disability?
2. What tasks does the service animal perform?

Businesses May Not:
1. Require special identification/certification
2. Ask about person's disability
3. Require task demonstration

If a dog poses a direct threat to others or is not under the control of the handler, the handler can be asked to remove the dog from the premises.

Questions? Call the ADA Info Line: 1-800-514-0301

Figure 9-2 shows an example that's customized to a particular state, in this case North Carolina. It cites the specific state statues for service animals. This can be very helpful because even police officers don't have every statute memorized and this card tells them exactly which laws apply.

Figure 9-2: Service Dog Information Card That Cites Statues

> North Carolina laws protect Service Dogs and their
> handlers just like federal law does, but the dog must
> be under control and not eliminate indoors, or the
> handler may legally be asked to remove the dog.
>
> www.PawsThenPlay.com
>
> § 168 4.2. (a)Every person with a disability has the
> right to be accompanied by a service animal trained
> to assist the person with his/her specific disability
> § 168 -4.4 A person with a disability accompanied
> by a service animal may not be required to pay any
> extra compensation for the animal

In accordance with the Americans with Disabilities Act of 1990

Businesses may ask:
1. Is this a Service Animal required because of a disability?
2. What work or tasks does this Service Animal perform?

Businesses may NOT:
1. Ask about the persons disability
2. Require identification or certification for the dog
3. Charge additional fees because of the dog
4. Refuse entry, isolate, segregate, or treat this person less favorably than other patrons.

NC Department of Health and Human Services 919-733-0390
US Department of Justice, Civil Rights Division 800-514-0301

A basic "I'm sorry, I can't talk to you right now, but here's a card," will get you off the hook almost every time.

Equipping Your Dog

In addition to readying yourself, you can prepare your dog to effectively manage public encounters. Your two biggest allies are your dog's appearance and trained commands. Unlike other people's behavior, these are both things you have control over.

Dressing for Success

Legally you don't have to vest your dog or do anything else that identifies it as a service dog. You can work your dog naked without breaking any laws as long as you aren't naked also. However, if your plan for the day includes passing through areas dogs aren't typically allowed, clearly and professionally identifying your dog as a service animal will save you a lot of hassle. It's also a form of being considerate - a gatekeeper can see at a glance that your dog is a service dog and may not even bother to ask. It also helps the management of the place you are visiting because it clearly identifies to other people present why a dog is being allowed in a no-pets space.

There is all manner of apparel that can be used to accomplish this, ranging from vests to collars to leash wraps or even a simple bandana marked "Service Dog." Vests are the most universally recognized of these and really all you need is a basic vest with patches saying "Service Dog" and perhaps a few additional patches of your choice. If you throw a pink camo tactical vest with 13 patches on your dog, you're asking for attention first and respect second. For starters, people are going to have to approach to read all those patches!

The urge to gussy up a plain old vest might be tempting, but before you get carried away, take a deep breath and remember: Your service dog is not a fashion accessory, it is a medical aid. If you don't want people to stare at you or pepper you with comments about your dog's wardrobe, keep it simple and professional. Otherwise the message - Service Dog: Do Not Distract - is likely to get lost in the glitz.

If your dog's vest has pockets, consider stocking them with a printout of *Frequently Asked Questions about Service Animals and the ADA*, which you can find in the appendix or online (**www.ada.gov/regs2010/service_animal_qa.html**). If you face an access challenge that threatens to go beyond the two questions allowed under federal law, this can be of help. You can also call it up on a smartphone. It's unlikely you'll need these but if you are a person who likes a little extra backup, this FAQ can provide some.

Finally, if you want to add a little drive-by-petting deterrent to your medium-to-large SD, consider adding a prong collar to your dog's wardrobe. This is strictly for appearance (unless you actually need one of these) and doesn't even need to be connected to a leash. Handlers who do this report it cuts down drive-by petting noticeably.

Handy Commands for Evading Pushy People

You can train your dog to ignore people who approach. The dog should really be doing this anyway, but paying no attention to people standing nearby is not nearly as challenging as ignoring a human who is actively offering to pet you and typically requires extra work - how much depends on the personality of the dog. Ensuring your dog is trained on the following commands will help.

- ✓ **Focus** - When you give the verbal command or cue, your SD should stop all other activity and look you in the eyes.

- ✓ **Leave it** - This very useful command informs your dog that something is off limits. Whatever is drawing its attention, whether a gushy person or a tasty treat dropped on the floor, must be left untouched.

- ✓ **Ignore** - Effectively the same as leave it, some handlers use this command for people because it sends a message to the intruding person at the same time.

If you have a bit of a devious side, consider coming up with a fake name for your dog and giving that one out in reply to unwanted prying. It's much easier for your dog to ignore someone who isn't calling it by name than someone who is. Don't try this if it's going to make you feel dishonest or awkward because you'd just be trading one discomfort for another. You can even take this a step farther and train this fake name as a command your dog will recognize. For example, you might train your dog to move behind you and lie down when you say the fake name.

Dealing with Drive-bys

A drive-by occurs when someone just jumps right in and interacts with your dog without your permission. Drive-by petting is the most common form - a hand reaches in from nowhere and starts stroking your dog inches away from the Do Not Pet patch. Your immediate reaction might by to say "Hey, what are you doing?"

and it's fine to go with that, moving out of reach at the same time. "Please don't do that, she's working," is a bit friendlier. Also try employing the ignore and leave it commands; half the time the drive-by petter will assume you're talking to them and draw back in shock. If you're feeling talkative, you can explain that loving on your dog while it's working interferes with its ability to perform its job, and reassure them there's plenty of petting when not on-duty.

Drive-by photographers are harder to deal with. Believe it or not, sometimes a complete stranger will snap a photo or video of you and your dog. Sometimes you'll be aware they've done it, but if it's done from across the room you may never know. You have no control over where they post it, what they say about it, or who they show it to. So frustrating and unnerving!

There's also not much you can do about it. It's rude but not illegal. If you catch them in the act, consider taking a picture of them right back and offering to delete yours if they delete theirs. This alone may get the point across. Plus, there are occasional bad people out there who take pictures for reasons other than because your dog is so handsome, and the fact that you've got their face recorded may dissuade them. Many people file drive-by photographers into the pick-your-battles folder and just ignore it and keep going. Chances are their motives are benign. Know it may happen, especially if you have an unusual service dog, but try not to sweat it. It's just one thing you have to deal with if you want to take your service dog to public places.

Handling an Access Challenge

If someone questions your right to bring your service dog into their establishment, it's referred to as an access challenge. If this does happen to you, most likely it will be a minor event:

> Gatekeeper: *Dogs aren't allowed in here!*

> You: *He's a service dog.* (as you keep walking)

> Gatekeeper: *Oh, okay.*

And you go on your merry way. Occasionally, however, you might run into more substantial resistance and have to put forth greater effort to overcome it. This can feel very intimidating even though you know the laws and are certain you're in the right, and it's a scary prospect for many new handlers. The truth is that access challenges are something everyone hears about but only a few encounter - especially if you follow the other advice in this chapter. Still, it's a good idea to have a plan for how you'll handle one if it occurs.

Working the Process

First, don't freak out. This isn't personal; it's just someone trying to do what they think they're supposed to do. It's a misunderstanding you can probably sort out, not a battle to the death. The gatekeeper may know the laws and think you don't look like you qualify (consider this a compliment on how healthy you look!), think the laws don't apply to their establishment, or simply not know them. While most people know service dogs are allowed in public places, many incorrectly think they have to wear a special vest, be "certified," or have "papers." Inform the gatekeeper that this is your service dog, which helps you with a disability, and the Americans with Disabilities Act requires them to allow you in.

At this point they will either let you pass or tell you that you don't look disabled, ask if you are blind even though obviously you are not, or ask you the second permitted ADA question: What work or tasks does your dog perform?

If your disability is not apparent, they have a legal right to ask the last question, but not the first two. Whichever they ask, answer as if they asked the legal question and give a succinct description of the work/task(s) your SD performs.

If you carry information cards or a handout with information about the ADA and/or state service dog laws, pull it out and hand it over. "Here, this explains the laws" or offer to pull up the information on a smartphone.

They might instead (or next) ask you for an ID, and if they do that it means they don't know what the law is and you'll have to decide if you want to attempt to educate them on the spot or let it go, at least temporarily.

If you're getting nowhere with the gatekeeper, before you give up, ask to see a manager. Even if the person working the door doesn't know the laws, the manager may. If you don't end up with an immediate apology and get sent about your business, repeat the previous steps with the manager. Ask them to educate their employee.

At any point you can opt to attempt to educate the person barring your progress or walk away and either follow up later or just go somewhere else. There are few things so imperative that you must solve them immediately or else, including this. You may actually have greater success resolving the problem from a distance later on, when you're feeling less heated.

Veronica Morris, PhD., President of Psychiatric Service Dog Partners (PSDP), has been a service dog handler since 2005. She's faced a few access confrontations over the years. At first they made her cry, she admits, but not anymore. She gives some excellent advice in an article titled "How I Handle a Public Access Challenge," which is available on the PSDP web site (**www.psychdogpartners.org**). One of her key bits of wisdom:

> *"...during any of these exchanges, I will be continuing on my way in the store, acting like I have every right to be there. If you stand there, orient your body toward them, and have a conversation with them, they are more likely to want to keep you in a longer fight about this. If you keep moving at a normal pace, they will usually give up pretty quickly and let you be."*

If Working the Process Doesn't Work

If things have become heated or your explanations just aren't getting through, it may just be your best option to hand over the number for the ADA hotline and leave the premises. You can follow up later, or even file a civil suit in federal court. It's not a bad idea to also whip out your cell phone and record the person insisting that you leave. Ask them "Are you refusing access to me and my service dog?" and get it all on video so you have proof they're kicking you out. Let them see you do it so they know they won't be able to deny the facts later and so you can't be accused of secretly recording a conversation, which is illegal in some places. Then leave.

Once outside, find a place to sit and calm yourself, and take copious notes. Record details, including date, time, location, taxi/bus/store#, names, and details of what happened. You can use these later if you decide to pursue the matter further.

You might be wondering if you should call the police at this point. The fact is that usually local police aren't much help with an access challenge. The ADA is a federal civil law. That means the local police can't enforce it, only federal courts can.

Some states have local statues that will cover you. In such places it may be worthwhile to phone the cops, but if you do, be sure when you call to tell them the number of the state statue that's being violated. That gives them time to look it up on the way over, as they may not be familiar with it.

You might also be wondering if now is the time to go online and bring down the social media hammer. Boy, won't they be sorry they messed with you! As tempting as it is, this is generally not recommended if your goal is to solve the problem and prevent it from happening again rather than punish them for being jerks. You can always come back and do this later if you really must.

Instead, go up the food chain. If you didn't get to talk to the store manager, try calling from home later. Contact the company's corporate headquarters or parent organization. Explain your civil rights as a disabled person were violated and ask them to educate their employees and correct the situation. If you meet any reluctance, this is a reasonable time to throw in an or-else. "or else I'm going to pursue this further" may well be good enough without getting specific.

Most likely you'll get a profuse apology and retraining will occur. If you don't receive a satisfactory resolution, you can still take your case to social media or even file a civil suit, if it's worth it to you.

Being a Service Dog Advocate

People who have service dogs are in a unique position to educate and inform others about them, but you don't have to be a service dog advocate just because you have a service dog. Even if you're shy, however, there are things you can do from the privacy of your home that can have a positive impact.

- ✓ **Keep an eye on proposed service dog legislation at the state level.** It often includes regulations based on misinformation that will negatively impact PSD handlers. You can contact legislators to oppose or support legislation and make a real difference. The Psychiatric Service Dog Partners (PSDP) website is a good place to watch for new service dog legislation across the U.S. - they watch for it themselves and comment on it. The exact page may move around, but look for their advocacy page.

- ✓ **Correct negative assumptions when you encounter them.** For example if someone compliments your "therapy dog," gently explain the difference.

- ✓ **Donate money to support nonprofit service dog organizations.** If your employer has a donation matching program, be sure to use it! If you shop at Amazon.com, start at smile.amazon.com instead of the standard amazon.com home page. From there you can select a charitable organization to support, after which Amazon will donate a portion of the price of items you purchase to that organization. This doesn't affect the price you pay and is a painless way to donate.

- ✓ **Volunteer to be a forum administrator.** Once you are thoroughly versed and confident of the legal and ethical aspects of service dog ownership, consider volunteering to help administer a Facebook group or other service dog forum. These groups are often in need of additional, knowledgeable assistance, as they are overwhelmed by new members and growing interest and must constantly defend against spammers.

Above all, when you're out with your dog, go about your day professionally. When people see your well-behaved service dog at your side, being unobtrusive and doing its job, they will have a positive picture of service dogs to remember.

Dealing with "Fakers"

You've probably heard about them in the news or online - those unethical people who claim their pet is a service dog so that they can bring it somewhere pets are not allowed. People who do that are in the wrong and breaking the law. They're also extremely rare. Still, spotting a poorly behaved "service dog" is sure to set your teeth on edge. You're following the rules and doing everything right but they're not. Perhaps you're worried they'll give service dogs a bad reputation that legitimate teams will pay for later. But here's the thing - how does an observer know for certain that another team is deliberately "faking it?"

First, you frequently cannot tell if someone has a disability by looking at them. Many disabilities are invisible.

Secondly, if it's the dog's appearance or behavior that has you questioning the team's authenticity, consider that service dogs are not robots, and even a well-trained dog can have an off day. Also, not all service dogs are professionally trained, and the disabled handler may be struggling with some aspect of training - that doesn't make them a faker. Or they might simply be wrong - for example thinking it's okay to put their tiny diabetic alert dog in a shopping cart when it isn't. Or maybe they have an ID clipped on their dog's vest - not because they believe in fake IDs but because it gets more people to leave them alone.

Confronting the suspected faker is a bad idea. If it is a legitimate team having an off day, you're just going to make it worse by acting like the Service Dog Police. If it is a genuine faker, it's best to keep your distance and let the management of the establishment you're in deal with it. If you're deeply concerned, approach management and share your concerns with them. Make sure they know the laws and that they can expel dogs who don't meet them. Then go on your way.

Playing Service Dog Bingo

On days where it seems like everybody who ever owned a dog, met a dog, or dreamt about one, wants to ask about your service dog and you're starting to get a headache, conditions are perfect for a game of service dog Bingo. Although you can play it solo, it's the most fun with multiple players. Figure 9-3 is a sample Service Dog

Bingo card. Use this card or make your own, carry it with you (you'll need pen or pencil too), and you're ready to play. Cross out each square as it occurs. Get five in a row across, down, or diagonally, yell BINGO! and you win.

Figure 9-3: Service Dog Bingo

B	*I*	*N*	*G*	*O*
You educate someone about service dogs	Won't you be sad when you give him/her up?	Why do you need a service dog?	You're so lucky you can bring your dog everywhere!	Where can I get a service dog vest like that?
How can I make my dog a service dog and take it everywhere?	I had a dog just like that but he died.	Dog tucks so well no one never even knew dog was there.	Pets without asking	You don't look blind /disabled.
You run an entire errand and no one asks about your dog	Makes kissy noises at your dog	FREE SPACE	Someone follows you around store	How can I get a service dog for my relative?
Who are you training him/her for?	Access challenge	Your dog ignores another dog that's behaving badly.	Someone is afraid of dogs	You hear a parent educating their child about SDs
Off leash dog runs up to your SD	Does he ever get to be normal dog?	Someone takes your dog's picture.	You spot a "service dog" in a shopping cart	Your dog completely ignores food dropped on ground

Chapter 10

Out and About with Your Service Dog

In this chapter

➤ Everyday guidelines to make your outings go smoothly

➤ Tips for taking transportation and staying in hotels

➤ Bringing your service dog to doctor appointments and even to the hospital

➤ Going to restaurants, movie theaters, and other fun places as a team

---

Becoming a confident service dog handler is a learning process. At first every place you go as a team will be a new experience. You will have questions about what to do with your dog in certain settings or during particular activities or even whether you should forgo teamwork and go solo. This chapter provides tips and advice on navigating common settings from handlers who have been there before.

The first tip, which carries across all settings, is to conduct yourself professionally as you go about your daily activities. While that sounds kind of serious, it isn't a demand for rigid perfection but rather a goal of presenting yourself in a way that encourages people to take you seriously and not pepper you with questions or intrusions into your personal life. At the simplest, it means your dog should be leashed, dressed in a service dog vest and firmly under your control at all times. Legally your dog doesn't have to be vested or visibly identified as a service animal, but practically speaking it will spare you and those around you significant hassle, and, well, it's just courteous. The goal is to smooth your way without disrupting anyone else's day. This is a service dog at your side, not a pet.

The second general guideline to keep in mind is that you alone are responsible for handling your service dog and meeting its needs. No one else is required to provide water for your dog or hold the leash while you do something, and you should count on managing those things yourself. If you won't be able to care for your dog yourself, then you should bring along a helper or leave your dog home. If your dog may need water, bring some along. Try to avoid the need for potty breaks and reduce the chance of accidents by encouraging your dog to go to the bathroom before any outing, but always keep poop bags in your pocket or your dog's vest and clean up any "deposits" immediately.

Following the two guidelines above will create a foundation for successful outings of all kinds. The rest of this chapter focuses on advice for specific destinations and situations. It's helpful to read through the whole chapter, but you can also opt to refer to particular sections as you need them.

Everyday Encounters

You probably use escalators, elevators, stairs, and public restrooms without a second thought. When you first go out with your service dog, you may find you suddenly have questions about the best way to manage your dog in these formerly routine places. The good news is that while you may need to pay extra attention the first few times you ride an elevator or venture into a public restroom with your service dog, these activities will quickly become routine once again. The most common questions are addressed in this section.

Navigating Escalators, Elevators & Stairs

When you're out and about with your service dog, it's pretty likely you'll also be going up and down to reach different levels of a structure. Escalators should be avoided because they pose a potential hazard to your partner. Toenails can get stuck between the moving steps and torn out and various bits of fur may get entrapped. You cannot train your way out of these possibilities. If there's an escalator, there's an elevator and/or stairs nearby; opt for one of those instead.

Elevators are a good option. Your dog should follow you onto an elevator, not the other way around, and the same holds true when getting off. This is standard procedure for all doorways and thresholds, so make sure your dog knows to wait and allow you to go first in such situations. Once inside, your dog should sit or stand at your side and ignore the other people on board. In a crowded elevator, you can make it a little easier for your dog by positioning yourself alongside a wall, with your dog between you and the wall and you between your dog and other people. Remember: some people are truly frightened of dogs, allergic to them, or wish to avoid them for religious reasons. Be especially respectful of these possibilities in a small, enclosed area like an elevator.

Stairs are another good choice. Going up and down them may seem like a no-brainer as long as you're physically able, but there are two things to keep in mind when your service dog is with you. First and foremost, your partner should stay beside you and not rush ahead or lag behind, either of which may throw you off balance. Some dogs have a natural tendency to run up stairs, just like children, but a service dog should be trained to go up or down at your speed. Second, take a moment to gather up any spare slack in the leash. A nice loose-leash walk is a beautiful thing on the sidewalk, but on a staircase it can be a hazard. With these things under control, navigating stairs with your service dog should be a breeze.

Deterring Dog Thieves

The thought of someone snatching away a service dog from a person who needs it is hard to fathom; after all, who would do such a heartless thing? The sad truth is that, while rare, service dog theft does occur. According to the American Kennel Club (AKC), dog theft of all kinds is on the rise. Purebred and/or highly trained dogs are attractive to a thief, who sees dollar signs instead of a desperately needed helper. They may sell the dog or even hold it for ransom. Dogs have been abducted from backyards, automobiles, and training facilities. Handlers have even reported instances of thieves attempting to wrest a leash from their hands. While it seems impossible to contemplate, contemplate it we must. Cut down your risk of becoming a victim by taking these precautions:

- Microchip your dog at the earliest opportunity. A collar with tags can be removed but a   microchip is invisible and inaccessible to the thief.

- Don't leave your dog unattended in your yard, especially if it's visible from the street.

- Avoid leaving your dog in the car alone. Even if it's locked, access is only a window-bash away.

- Be wary of anyone who probes for lots of information about your dog, especially if they start asking about cost or where you live.

- If the worst happens and your dog is stolen, you can increase the chances of recovery by acting quickly, starting with the following steps:

- Call the police immediately and file a report. Make sure you give them the microchip info. Call animal control, too.

- Contact local media online and over the phone and ask them to publish a story about the theft. Provide a recent picture and a description of the circumstances under which your dog was stolen.

- Canvas the neighborhood where the theft occurred, asking questions in case anyone saw something relevant. Put up posters with your dog's picture and your contact info.

- Check animal shelters around where the theft occurred.

- Set up profiles on sites such as PetFinder.com and

FindFido.com.

- Monitor pet-for-sale and pet adoption ads for descriptions matching your dog.

- Don't give up hope. Lost and stolen animals are sometimes recovered.

Service dog theft is far from an everyday occurrence, and there's no need to work yourself into a state of hypervigilant paranoia over the possibility, but it is important to be aware and take reasonable precautions.

Utilizing Public Restrooms

Everybody has to pee sooner or later, and chances are you'll need to visit public restrooms during outings. Your service dog can go right in with you. If the stall is big enough, bring your service dog inside it; otherwise, it can remain just outside the door in a sit or stand, but only if coming in with you is truly impractical. Feel free to use the handicapped stall to gain extra space; it's not limited to wheelchair users.

Since bathroom floors can be rather yucky, it's best to have your dog in a stand-stay or sit rather than a full down. Many dogs don't know stand-stay, but this is a good reason to train it. Even if you're certain your partner will stay put, keep the leash looped over your wrist or otherwise attached to you.

Hitting the Road (or the Friendly Skies)

Taking a service dog on public transportation can be one of the more nerve-wracking experiences for new handlers. Rest assured that service dogs are permitted by federal laws to travel on public transportation with you. The law that applies will vary depending on the type of transportation, but pretty much all forms are covered by one law or another. If you're travelling to another country or to an island such as Hawaii, be sure to check the regulations at your destination as they may be different than those in the continental U.S. For example, some destinations require incoming animals to go through a quarantine period on arrival. In addition, laws regarding service dogs vary substantially among countries. Some may not recognize psychiatric service dogs or owner-trained service dogs or may require some form of certification for any service dog.

Travelling by Air

Thanks to the Air Carrier Access Act (ACAA), your service dog or emotional support dog can travel in the passenger area of an airplane with you. The airport itself is covered by the ADA. Both laws are explained in detail in Chapter 7: Knowing Service Dog Laws. Being aware of the pertinent regulations isn't going to help you know what it's like to pass through security or board an airplane with a service dog, but this section will help with that. The primary keys to success are planning ahead and knowing what to expect.

Before You Leave Home

Check with the airline ahead of time and notify them you will be travelling with a service animal (or emotional support animal if your dog is still in training). Don't ask for permission; just inform them that you are accompanied by a service dog. If your dog is travelling as a psychiatric service dog or emotional support animal, you'll need to provide documentation from a medical professional, as described in Chapter 7: Knowing Service Dog Laws. On most airplanes bulkhead seating typically offers more floor room, but not always. Window seats are better because they keep your dog away from the aisle, where it might get stepped on or tripped over. Plus you won't have to get up to let other travellers in and out of the row. Try to schedule a direct flight whenever possible so you don't have to deal with layovers.

Another thing to verify in advance is whether the airports you'll be passing through have dedicated pet relief areas, and if so, where they are in relation to your airline's gates. In the past, most airport pet relief areas were outside security, with only a few having potty areas inside security, but thanks to a 2015 U.S. Department of Transportation ruling, that has changed. As of August 2016, all but the smallest airports (those with under 10,000 passengers annually) must provide a pet relief area in each terminal. Don't expect freshly mown grass and a park bench though; a patch of fake turf and a decorative fire hydrant are more the norm. Limit food and water for several hours before the flight and you may not even need to visit one. Skip meals within eight hours of the flight and limit water starting two hours in advance. It won't hurt your service dog and will make her more comfortable.

If possible, exercise your dog the day before and day of your flight. It will be easier for her to lie still if she's burned off some of that endless energy. Make sure she is clean and well-groomed and won't be leaving a trail of dog hair along the way.

It's not necessary to haul along your entire supply of dog stuff on every trip, but be sure to bring along these essentials in your carry on:

- ✓ poop bags
- ✓ a collapsible water bowl or small cup for water
- ✓ small treats
- ✓ ADA service dog cards if you have them
- ✓ optionally, a small blanket or towel for your dog to lie on
- ✓ optionally, a serving of dog food in case your checked luggage gets lost or delayed

Don't play with your dog while waiting for your flight. Focus on calm, settled behavior. If your dog is a full service dog, you can bring it into eating and retail establishments in the airport. If it's still in training and travelling as an emotional support animal, businesses are not legally required to permit access, although they may not object.

What to Expect from Airport Security

You will have to pass through security screening just as you would without a service dog. Typically you'll be asked to step through the detector yourself, while your dog waits, and then the dog will come follow after you and be screened separately. TSA staff can't require you to remove your dog's leash, vest, or collar during this process, though you may need to remove the contents of any vest pockets and send those through the scanner separately. You won't be permitted to carry water through security, so plan to buy bottled water once inside.

You and your dog may be sent through a metal detector instead of the scanner. Some handlers opt to use a collar with a plastic buckle while travelling so it won't set off the detector. Alternatively, you can temporarily remove your dog's collar and use a slip-lead that won't set off the alarm. If the alarm does go off, it's not a big deal; it just means that your dog will have to be patted down or wanded. If that happens, talk to your dog in an encouraging tone and try to keep her attention on you to reduce the likelihood she'll get flustered and squirmy. You can help prepare your dog by making sure it she is comfortable being handled and touched all over, not only by you but by other people.

Boarding the Plane & During the Flight

You may ask for or be offered early boarding, but if you don't have a mobility impairment you can just board when your zone is called. Early boarding gives you a chance to get your dog settled, which can be especially helpful if you have a large dog. If you have a large dog, you may need to back her into the row instead of send her in head first. You can practice this at home by setting up your furniture to simulate a narrow aisle, such as setting a coffee table alongside a couch, then practicing having your dog back into the space. Small and medium dogs can walk into the seating row head first and curl partially beneath the seat in front, where you would otherwise stow carryon luggage. If your dog is used to lying on a towel or blanket, place it on the floor where you want her to stay. Get your dog to tuck (i.e. curl up small) to avoid intruding your neighboring passenger's foot space. If your dog isn't already good at tucking, practice before your flight.

Encourage your dog to settle and don't fuss over her. Ideally she will sleep throughout the flight or at least lay quietly. The vibrations and other sensations during take-off and landing are disturbing to some dogs, and if yours is one of them, distract her by feeding a few small treats and offer reassurance. Your service dog should remain on the floor, not on a seat or in your lap. As always, think business-like, not pet-like, when setting behavior expectations for yourself and your dog. Aircraft restrooms are tiny, so try to avoid the need to use them by utilizing facilities in the airport shortly before take-off. If you have to go, asking a travelling companion to hold your dog's leash until your return is the first choice; otherwise, you'll need to squeeze into the bathroom together as flight attendants aren't required to help you out by managing your dog while you do your business.

Once you reach your destination and pick up your luggage, immediately toilet your dog and provide water and a short walk.

Taking a Taxi, Train, or Bus

Few people would list taking public transportation on their list of fun things to do, and adding a service dog into the mix can compound the stress. By law, service dogs are permitted to accompany you in taxis and on trains and busses. You may encounter resistance because drivers and personnel are not always acquainted with these laws and just see a pet, not a service dog, boarding their vehicle. However, rest assured, you are allowed to be accompanied by your service dog. At the same time, it's important to be respectful of other passengers, who might be afraid of dogs or want to avoid them for religious reasons.

To ensure the path of least resistance, vest your dog and conduct yourself in a routine, matter-of-fact manner. Once on board, position your dog in an unobtrusive spot, out of the flow of traffic. In a taxi, this means on the floor, never on the seat. In a bus or on a train, your dog should settle in your foot space or underneath your seat and stay there quietly until you reach your destination. You may wish to bring a small towel or pad for your dog to lie on, though it's not required. If your dog isn't able to settle like this, it's not ready for this type of public access and you should conduct more training before attempting it.

Uber is covered by the ADA even though drivers use their own cars. Legally, Uber drivers must allow a service dog to ride with its handler.

The ADA applies to rental cars. Although most rental car companies prohibit pets, a service dog is not a pet and must be allowed. You cannot be charged an extra fee for having your service dog, but if a mess that requires extra cleaning results, you can be charged for the clean-up. When renting a vehicle, you can help avoid potential problems by spreading a sheet or blanket over the entire area where your dog will ride.

When taking a long journey by bus or train, choose a run that includes intermediate stops and/or rest stops so that you can water and toilet your dog throughout the trip. Bring bottled water with you so you don't have to use up limited break time hunting it down.

Travelling by Car

Most dogs instantly hop in or out of a car when you open the door, but service dogs should be trained in what's referred to as controlled loading and unloading. Instead of leaping in or out automatically and willy-nilly, the dog should wait until you give permission. This is something you can easily practice at home and it's well worth the effort.

Whenever possible, your dog should be safely secured when travelling in a vehicle. Most of us don't really think about this - we just open the door and our dog hops in and off we go - but there are numerous ways such an innocent act can lead to disaster. If you're involved in an accident, your dog may be catapulted around the interior of the car and be seriously injured or killed. If emergency personnel open your vehicle to pull you out, your frightened dog may leap out onto to the road and be struck by a car or run off in confusion. Those are the dramatic worst-case scenarios you might think would never happen, but you aren't the only person on the road and an accident can happen no matter how careful of a driver you are. Even a fairly routine stomp of the brakes can send your dog flying off its comfy perch and into the dashboard or seatback.

It's also not uncommon for a dog to slip unnoticed out of a car door during a stop for gas or a bathroom break. You might not even notice it's happened until farther down the road when you turn to your partner and he's not there. If this happens you may never get him back. Why risk it?

There are several options for properly securing your dog in a car, but simply slipping a seatbelt through your dog's leash isn't one of them. Although that would keep your dog in the car, he would still fly off the seat, strike the interior, and in a serious crash quite possibly sustain a neck injury due to the sudden collar jerk. There are much better ways.

A safe method is to have your dog travel in an approved crate or carrier that is itself secured to the vehicle floor or seat. This contains your dog in a comfortable way while still allowing some movement. If you keep it set up in your regular vehicle, it's also easy - just open the door, in he goes, close the door and you're on your way. Travelling in a crate can also help prevent car sickness for dogs who suffer from it.

A crate isn't the only option. If you can't fit one in your vehicle or really want or need your canine partner closer at hand during travel, consider a restraint harness. A restraint harnesses fits on your dog like a regular harness but is designed to disburse the force of impact across a dog's chest and body where it will do the least damage. The harness is placed on the dog and connected to a buckled seatbelt by a short, strong tether. The dog can move about a little bit but is restrained to the seat. Some of these harnesses are designed for dual use as a walking harness. It's also very easy to use a harness in different vehicles with minimal hassle.

There are no industry standards or regulations regarding restraint harnesses or crates, so do your homework before purchasing. A widely circulated study performed in 2013 by the Center for Pet Safety revealed that many harnesses failed in an actual crash. A similar study was performed on crates in 2015, with similar results. Manufacturers seem to have taken heed and updated their products, so that 2013 study is pretty much outdated now, but it still serves as a reminder that you need to do some comparison shopping to find an appropriate harness or crate and not just grab one off the shelf.

If you love your service dog, secure it while in the car. It's that simple. Accidents occur in an instant and regrets last a lifetime. If you can't properly secure your dog for some reason, then the safest place for him to ride is on the floor in the back between seats or possibly in the foot well on the floor in front of the front passenger seat. Make it habit to secure your dog one way or another whenever possible, just as you automatically buckle in yourself or children.

Staying in a Hotel or Motel

You can always stick to pet-friendly lodging when travelling with your service dog, but you don't have to. Hotels are squarely on the list of places that must permit your service dog to accompany you, per the ADA. The hotel cannot charge you a pet fee for a service dog, even if they usually charge one for pet dogs. Nor can they restrict you to particular rooms.

If your dog is still in training, whether or not they can accompany you depends on which state the hotel is in. Some states grant the same access to service dogs in training as to service dogs, and in those states you can go to any hotel. In states that don't have such a law, you'll have to stick to pet-friendly lodging until your dog is full service dog.

Although hotel staff are supposed to treat a person accompanied by a service dog the same way they would treat someone who isn't, they don't always do that automatically. Sometimes they don't know the law; other times they just don't like it. There have even been reports of hotel staff informing handlers the hotel is full when it really isn't.

To get around such people, some handlers leave their dog in the car while they check in. You're also not legally required to mention that you have a service dog when making a reservation, and many handlers don't. If the staff kicks up a fit when the dog enters afterward, at least they've already got a room, making it harder to turn them away. If you encounter resistance like this, be prepared to educate. Hand over the ADA hotline number and ask for a manager if necessary. Threaten to file a complaint if you must.

The majority of hotels know they can't treat a person with a service dog differently, so as long as you don't present yourself in a way that makes them doubt the authenticity of your service dog, you probably won't have any problems. Large chain hotels are more likely to know the laws than a small mom-and-pop operation. With a hotel chain, you can always call the corporate office if you have a problem with the front desk staff, and they usually have a 24-hour customer service number so you can call no matter what time you encounter an issue.

If your dog damages the room in any way, you can be required to pay for repairs. They can't charge you a special cleaning fee though, or any other fee that is strictly because your dog is accompanying you.

Remember your side of the ADA - You must answer the two questions permitted by law if asked: Is this a service dog needed due to a disability and what work or tasks does it perform? Also, you can't leave your service dog in your room unattended while you go out. It must be under your direct control at all times.

Tending to Medical Care

For a lot of us, medical settings = stress. The waiting room is packed with strangers, and often from there you sit alone in a small room waiting for the provider to appear. The surroundings often include visual cues, sounds, and smells that can trigger anxiety in anyone, but especially in people who have mental health issues. Having your service dog at your side can make the situation much more tolerable.

Medical Appointments

You can legally bring your service dog with you to a medical appointment without informing the provider beforehand, and often that's what handlers do. However, it's not a bad idea to call ahead and mention you'll be accompanied by your trained service dog. Then if there's any resistance, you can clear it up in advance and not risk adding even more stress to your actual appointment.

It's important to consider what will happen during your appointment. Will you be getting x-rays or lab work? What will you do with your dog during that time? During lab work, your dog can probably lie nearby, but it can't be in the room during an x-ray. If there will be any reason you'll be unable to handle your dog yourself, bring along a helper or leave the dog home. The office staff are not required or expected to manage your dog for you and you shouldn't ask them to do so. Be certain your dog has a very solid down-stay so you can focus on the business that brought you to the office.

What about dental appointments? After all, just the dental office smell wafting out of the back rooms triggers many people, even before the drill starts whirring. Legally speaking, the answer is yes, because a dentist office is not considered a sterile environment as are some other places, like burn units and operating rooms. Practically speaking though, think about the size of the room where you'll be worked on. Is there a place for your dog where it won't be in the way? Often dental exam rooms are tiny and the answer is no, although sometimes there may be enough space on the floor, up against the base of the chair. Having your dog lay atop of you while the dentist works above with buzzing tools and suction hoses isn't advisable either; one wrong movement by your dog, and you could have a new hole in your lip! Here again, consider bringing a helper with you to remain with your dog in the waiting room, where it will still be nearby, or leave it at home.

Hospitals, Emergency Rooms & Ambulances

Service dogs are permitted to accompany their owners inside hospitals and emergency rooms except in areas that are considered sterile, such as operating rooms and the burn unit. Your service dog can come with you when you visit someone who is hospitalized or if you're seeking treatment yourself, outside of such areas.

It can be a great help to have your service dog during a trip to the ER, but it can also be a significant inconvenience. This is another one of those cases where just because you can, doesn't mean you should. What will you do with your dog if you need to be wheeled off for a CT scan or other procedure? You can't expect hospital staff to take care of him, so unless you have someone along who can take over managing your dog, you probably shouldn't bring him. If you're just going in for something relatively minor such as a few stitches, where you know what to expect, it's more reasonable to bring along your service dog, even if you're going alone. Also, although legally hospitals must let you bring your service dog, that doesn't mean they're going to be happy about it, so keep that in mind. One nurse might be thrilled about it while another is aggravated. Be prepared for it to go either way.

If you're admitted, your dog can stay with you in your room, but only if you are able to provide the care it needs. Realistically, if you're sick enough to be hospitalized, you're probably not going to be capable of taking your dog outside to potty several times a day and otherwise tending to its needs. If you're on a locked psychiatric unit, you can't go in and out even if you're physically able. A lucky few people have friends or relatives who can commit to coming to the hospital multiple times daily to tend to their dog, and if you can swing such an arrangement, your dog can stay in a hospital room with you. Otherwise, unfortunately, you'll have to make do with visits.

What about ambulances? If your dog is a service animal and it will fit safely in the ambulance, the ADA requires that the dog be allowed to ride in the ambulance with you. I hate to keep saying this but this is another case of can doesn't equal should. The back of an ambulance is a crowded, small, swaying space with potentially a lot going on. You will have medical experts taking care of you, so you probably can get by without your service dog for the duration of the ride.

All this talk about emergency rooms and ambulances and not bringing your service dog with you points out an important need - you should have a plan for caring for your service dog if/when you are unable to do so yourself. Find someone who can take care of your service dog in an emergency. Perhaps a family member, close friend, or if you received your dog from a program, a contact there, will agree to fill this important role. You may never need to call on them, but it's best to have a plan just in case. Keep contact information on a card in your wallet, in your cell phone's ICE list, and/or in a pocket of your dog's service vest so that you can use it yourself or provide it to an emergency responder. If you don't do this, it's possible your dog could end up unattended to at home or even sent to a shelter, a very unpleasant outcome.

Attending Recreational & Social Activities

As the old saying goes, "all work and no play makes Jack a dull boy." If you're like most PSD handlers, one of the key reasons for having a service dog is to be able to get out and do more things - fun things, social things, and recreational things. As you prepare to galavant about (or at least venture out) with your newfound freedom, you may find yourself wondering about the best ways to negotiate different environments with your service dog. This section offers advice on common destinations. Don't be a dull boy.

Dining Out

Eating out is about relaxing, having a good time, and, well, eating. It's very easy to take a service dog with you to a dining establishment. Any well-trained service dog can handle a restaurant environment with confidence if you follow a few simple guidelines.

First, place your dog under the table whenever possible. Booth seating is ideal for this, and a service dog tucked away at your feet will usually go unnoticed and undisturbed. If you can't get a booth, then still try to place your dog under the table, which ensures it isn't blocking the path of patrons or servers. If your SD is on the large side, you may need to get a four-person table for just two of you to accomplish this, but it's worth the effort. If your dog can't fit under the table, then place it in a down stay in the most out-of-the-way spot available, such as between your chair and a wall. A service dog, even a very small one, should never be allowed on the seating or in your lap in a restaurant. Always practice "four on the floor."

Don't put down a bowl of water or feed your dog under the table. When your dog is with you in an eating establishment, it's on duty, and the dog's focus should be on you, not dinner. If you like to feed your dog table scraps, save them for later. Rarely, a server may offer to provide your dog water or food, and in such cases it's best to politely decline: "No thanks, he's working right now. He already ate." Your dog should already be trained not to scarf up tasty tidbits from the floor, but if you see it happening, issue a firm "leave it" and don't permit the behavior to continue.

At buffet style restaurants, your service dog can accompany you through the serving line. If you don't have a hands-free style leash, balancing a plate, serving utensils, and a leash may require more hands than you possess, so it may be easier to enlist someone to go through the line with you and help serve your plate. You may also leave your dog at the table with a dining companion holding the leash, but never unattended.

Taking in a Movie

Going to a movie theater presents several challenges: lots of people, food and sticky stuff all over the floor, and potentially sudden loud noises from the sound track. The first time you take your service dog, it may wonder what in the world is going on, but there are things you can do to smooth the way:

- ✓ Bring a small towel or pad for your dog to lie on. Movie theater floors can be sticky, cold, and hard. Your dog should lie between the seat rows at your feet and not protrude into the aisle.

- ✓ Make sure your dog has a solid "leave it" command. Your dog shouldn't be snarfing up other people's dropped popcorn.

- ✓ Prepare yourself to fend off curious people and drive-by petters without becoming upset or anxious.

Some handlers put ear muffs on their pooch, but unless your dog is particularly sensitive to loud noises, that's really not necessary.

Going to Church

You might expect churches to be covered by the public access regulations of the ADA because after all, the general public is allowed into them, but they aren't. Religious organizations or entities controlled by religious organizations are legally exempt from the ADA. This means you can't just walk into church with your service dog the way you can walk into a business. There's a simple solution to this: just ask permission first. Most churches will willingly grant it. If not, you may need to find a different congregation.

During services, your dog should be in a down-stay at your feet or tucked beneath the pew if there's room. Before you attend, formulate a plan for how you will deal with people who want to pet your dog, because there will be many. Will you allow it or ask them not to? Over time this will become less of an issue as people learn your preferences, but the first time or two you should expect this and have a response in mind.

Working Out at the Gym

Service animals are legally permitted to accompany to your gym or fitness center, but they can't jump into the pool with you! Handlers who take their service dog to the gym report that they have the dog lie down and stay beside the equipment they are using. Of course take care that there are no moving parts or potentially dropped weights close by. During a class, your dog can rest out of the way alongside a nearby wall. Service dogs are allowed on the pool deck area but usually cannot go into the pool because the ADA does not override public health rules that prohibit dogs in swimming pools.

Hiking and Camping

It would be nice if the rules were the same everywhere, but when it comes to hiking and camping, the rules pertaining to service dogs vary depending on where you are. National parks, state parks, and private campgrounds can have slightly different rules, although all of them must permit you to be accompanied by your service animal. If the park doesn't allow pets, it's a good idea to keep your dog vested so it's apparent she's a service dog.

In national parks, service animals (but not service animals in training) are allowed in all facilities and on all trails except for areas that have been closed by the park superintendent to protect park resources. If you're planning to do any back country hiking, you may need to obtain a free service animal permit in advance. The park's website will usually contain instructions on how to obtain one. You can also call park headquarters and ask. In most national parks, your service dog will have to remain on leash and under your control at all times, even in isolated back country areas. Take the leash rules seriously; if your dog runs off after a squirrel or other animal, he can easily get lost, and a dog lost in the wilderness has little chance of being found again.

State parks generally have similar rules to national parks, but it's a good idea to call ahead to check. Some state parks require a rabies certificate or dog license for all dogs, whether they are service animals or not.

Private campgrounds can exclude pets, but they can't legally exclude your service dog or charge you an extra fee to have it along. The manager of a small or newer private campground might not be familiar with the laws, so it's best to call ahead and get the lay of the land. If necessary, you can educate them.

In addition to legal regulations, keep in mind these additional are guidelines for camping happiness:

- ✓ Make sure all vaccinations are up to date and deploy flea and tick protection of some kind.

- ✓ Many trails have no water resource, so be sure to bring plenty along. It's best not to let your dog drink from a stream or pond as it may ingest a parasite such as Giardia and end up with explosive diarrhea. Yuck!

- ✓ Never leave dog food out at your campsite. Keep it sealed in a tight container and stored where bugs, raccoons, and other wildlife will be unaware of its presence.

- ✓ Your dog should sleep in your tent at night as coyotes, wolves, and bears sometimes attack dogs. Skunks are often plentiful at campgrounds...

- ✓ You are required to pick up dog poop, even out in the middle of nowhere.

- ✓ Never leave your dog alone at your campsite. Not even for a few minutes.

This may seem like a lot of rules to remember, but none of them require a whole lot of work on your part, and the benefits of having your canine partner at your side are worth it.

Amusement Parks & Resorts

Yes, you can bring your service dog to Disney World. Public attractions such as amusement parks and resorts are subject to the ADA and its public access requirements. If the state the amusement park resides in grants access to service dogs in training (which Florida does as of this writing), then technically you could bring an SDiT as well (for training purposes), but with all the chaos that goes on in such places, it's really best to wait until your dog is fully trained. There will be crowds, food, smells, excited children, and distractions everywhere. It would be a shame to fork over the price of admission only to leave shortly thereafter because your SDiT can't handle it.

Your service dog can even accompany you on rides and attractions deemed to be safe. The dog will need to lie on the floor at your feet, not sit in your lap or on the seat beside you. For attractions where safety concerns prohibit service dogs, you'll either need to skip them or bring someone willing to wait with your SD while you ride.

It's always a good idea to check in with guest relations when you arrive. They can advise you on which attractions are accessible to you and your service dog and on any procedures that may facilitate your enjoyment of the park. Disney resorts, for example, have an alternate place you can wait to enter an attraction instead of in the default line. It won't get you to the ride any faster, but it will save you from standing in a long queue with your service dog. A few parks even have kennels at some rides where your service dog can wait for you, if you're comfortable leaving your dog.

Additional tips include:

- ✓ Ask facility staff where to take your dog to potty. Theme parks usually have specific locations identified for this purpose.

- ✓ Be prepared to fend off (or welcome) children and adults eager to pet your dog. They won't always ask first.

- ✓ Be alert for hot pavement, broken glass, or other footing conditions that might harm your dog's paws. Some handlers opt to use dog booties for protection. If you go this route, be sure to get your dog used to them in advance - and take a video - the first time a dog puts booties on can be pretty funny!

- ✓ Bring a collapsible bowl for water.

- ✓ Use your judgement in choosing rides. Even if service dogs are permitted it might be too much for your partner.

- ✓ Consider arriving shortly after the park opens as mornings are much less crowded than afternoons.

- ✓ During summer months, parks can get very hot. Make sure your dog isn't getting overheated.

With these tips in mind, your visit to a theme or amusement park should go smoothly.

There's something important to keep in mind wherever you go: If you can safely navigate places without your service dog, you aren't required to bring it with you. Many people benefit hugely from the work their service does right at home, and that's all they need. Others might initially plan to take their service dog everywhere but in practice find that the extra attention triggers too much anxiety to be worth it. Leaving your service dog home doesn't make it any less of a service dog or your needs any less legitimate, so choose what works best for you.

Chapter 11

Peering into the Future

In this chapter

➤ Using medical imaging to see how dogs think

➤ Harnessing the powers of the amazing canine nose

➤ Enhancing dog-human communication through wearable technology

➤ Ongoing research into service dogs for veterans

This book is all about current opportunities, laws, and social standards that allow people with invisible disabilities such as mental health impairments to partner with a service dog for better living. The Americans with Disabilities Act (ADA) explicitly covers service dogs for psychiatric disabilities, and members of society are becoming familiar with the concept of service dogs for mental health disabilities. Things are likely to get even better in the future.

Researchers and pet owners have always been interested in understanding how dogs think, but new tools and advanced medical imaging now allow researchers to observe the canine brain in action. In combination with developing technologies, that's leading to new ways that humans and dogs can work together. In parallel, scientists are designing formal studies seeking quantitative confirmation that service dogs can benefit people with mental health problems like post-traumatic stress disorder and others. That means there may soon be hard numbers to go with all the personal stories of dramatic impact. This chapter explores exciting work that's going on right now.

Peeking Inside the Canine Mind

Researchers around the world are investigating the inner workings of the canine mind through the use of functional MRI scanning (fMRI). An fMRI scanner can reveal the brain's response to specific stimuli by indicating which areas of the brain are active. The researchers can witness neurological responses to things like praise or particular odors. Similarities and differences between dogs can be identified and compared. In fact, one of the first things revealed is that big differences exist, both within a single breed and across breeds. For example, some dogs' brains react uniformly to praise from anyone but others show a distinct difference to praise from their owner versus praise from a friendly stranger.

This type of research has taken off since researchers discovered that dogs can be trained to willingly lie still through the noisy, claustrophobic process of being scanned in an MRI machine. Previously dogs were sedated and restrained or anesthetized before scanning, which nixed the possibility of observing their brains' natural actions but was thought to be the only way to ensure the dog would lie still. Gregory Berns, M.D., Ph.D. of Emory University, thought differently, and he ended up pioneering this new approach with his own dog in his quest to glimpse the inner workings of the canine brain.

In 2014, Auburn University and iK9, a provider of detection and service dogs, received a million dollar grant from the U.S. Defense Advanced Research Project Agency (DARPA) to work with and develop this technology under a research project dubbed FIDOS, which is an acronym for Functional Imaging to Develop Outstanding Service Dogs. Phase one includes a plan to "explore the feasibility of cognitive neuroscience and imaging experimental procedures for examining qualities indicative of a dog being an exemplary candidate for working tasks and TBI/PTSD therapeutic roles," or in other words, to identify dogs likely to excel at this work. They also plan to attempt to identify cognitive markers in dogs who are likely to excel at scent detection tasks. Imagine if you could identify dogs that possess an ideal mentality for service work

AND could likely be trained to sniff out signs of stress such as an increased cortisol level?

The relationship between Auburn and iK9 is neither entirely philanthropic nor focused on service dogs for disabled individuals, as the two also have licensing agreements related to training and selling explosive detection dogs. Hopefully they will maintain significant focus on the service dog aspects as well.

Additional canine research centers and service dog organizations are also in on the hunt to identify patterns of canine cognition that signify suitability for particular work, such as service work for a disabled handler. Among them are The Duke Canine Cognition Center of Duke University and the service dog organization Canine Companions for Independence (CCI), which are working to build on Gregory Berns' work and seek out biomarkers that identify dogs with ideal traits for specific types service work, also using fMRI.

Success by either or both efforts could remove the guess work from selecting service dog candidates. Canine cognitive imaging research like this is packed with exciting possibilities.

Sniffing Out Stress

Diabetic alert dogs are trained use their fantastic sense of smell to detect infinitesimally faint odors that indicate changes in their owner's blood sugar level. No one knows how dogs that detect impending seizures do so, but it's suspected that their amazing noses might have something to do with that, too. In both of these examples, the dog warns the owner of a looming problem so the owner can take action and head off a bad outcome. What if dogs could inform us that our stress level is rising before we even become aware of it?

Already some psychiatric service dogs are trained to pick up on early signs of anxiety, such as jiggling legs or skin picking, and to alert their owner by nudging or pawing, but not everyone displays visible signs of stress or perhaps not until they're far down the road toward a panic attack. What if your service dog's amazing nose could smell your stress level go up and it could respond by notifying you or comforting or distracting you?

Cortisol is a hormone that's linked to stress levels in human beings. When stress increases, our adrenal glands release cortisol into the bloodstream, and our cortisol level goes up. As the stress subsides, it drops down. Dogs can smell cortisol, and they can be trained to respond to it. There are multiple reports of successful efforts to train dogs to react to changes in their handler's cortisol level. If dogs can smell stress, can they also smell other emotions? Probably so, but someone still needs to figure out how to train dogs to do so and what to do with the resulting information. It's an exciting frontier well worth keeping an eye on.

Wearable Computing for Service Dogs

Computer technology isn't just migrating from our desktops to our pockets and wrists and even elements of everyday apparel, it's also going to the dogs. Since 2013, Georgia Institute of Technology researchers have been developing a "smart" backpack that enables dogs to trigger sophisticated actions at will. By activating sensors in the vest, the dog can call 911 through the handler's cell phone, send a text message, or play an audio recording to communicate important information, such as "my handler needs you to come with me!"

The system is under ongoing development at Georgia Tech's Animal Computer Interaction lab as part of project FIDO (**fido.gatech.edu**), which stands for "facilitating interactions for dogs with occupations." Early prototypes were built using an inexpensive, commercially available programmable microprocessor platform called Arduino, a favorite of hobbyists and tinkerers.

Challenges such as cost, durability, and battery life must be addressed before such vests will come into practical use, but it's certainly interesting to think about and watch develop.

Studying Service Dogs for PTSD

The U.S. Veterans Administration (VA) is in the midst of a study on the effectiveness of service dogs in treating post-traumatic stress disorder (PTSD). While there are plenty of stories and anecdotal evidence supporting this use, the VA wants hard, clinical numbers before embarking down the path of providing service dogs to veterans with mental health disabilities. This study originally commenced in 2011 but was suspended twice due to problems carrying it out. It's back on again and scheduled to conclude in 2018. Hopefully it will provide the evidence the VA is seeking before prescribing service dogs for veterans with PTSD, but the design of the study isn't without controversy, and it's far from a sure thing.

In an effort to make uniform, controlled comparisons possible, the study requires, among other things, that each dog placed with a veteran be trained on particular tasks. These include blocking to create a buffer zone around the handler and sweeping a room for security before the handler enters. Questions have arisen around whether these tasks actually perpetuate the hypervigilance that accompanies PTSD rather than work to alleviate it. Would it be more helpful in the long run for the service dog instead to pick up behavioral cues from its handler and respond in a way that helps calm the handler rather than act as if the threats the handler fears might actually be present - in other words, to respond to actual events rather than perceived threats? If service dogs in this study make veterans more able to go out and about but don't actually improve their PTSD, will the study be considered a success or failure?

It's impossible to predict how the findings of this study will be interpreted and put to use. Hopefully it will result in an ongoing program to provide service dogs to veterans suffering from PTSD. In the meantime, veterans will have to continue to use other means, such as going through nonprofit service dog providers and owner training.

The VA isn't the only entity trying to develop quantitative evidence on the use of service dogs for PTSD treatment in veterans. Using a grant from the Human Animal Bond Research Initiative Foundation, researchers at Purdue University Veterinary College are conducting a study on the use of service dogs for post 9-11 veterans who suffer from PTSD or traumatic brain injury. To assess effectiveness, the study will use three indicators:

1) Medical indicators (medication use and number of doctor visits)

2) Physiological indicator (salivary cortisol awakening response)

3) Self-perception (standardized self-report instruments from other PTSD treatment research to assess quality of life, including anxiety, self-efficacy, suicidal thinking, and family reintegration)

While these studies focus and others like them focus on veterans, the results will benefit people who have PTSD from causes other than war as well.

Changing Legislation

While federal laws trump state laws, state laws still matter. An increasing number of states are updating legislation that affects service dog handlers in positive ways. For example, although the ADA specifically recognizes psychiatric service dogs, many older state laws only reference service dogs for physical disabilities. The ADA still applies in such cases, but when the state provides additional regulations, such as permitting a service dog in training to go the same places a full service dog is permitted, it's important that the state's definition includes service dogs of all kinds.

In another spreading legislative development, more states are adding regulations that make it illegal to misrepresent a dog as a service dog when it isn't. This should help cut down on people taking untrained dogs into public places, claiming they are service dogs, and setting a poor standard of performance that can have a negative impact on people who have actual service dogs. The ADA doesn't address that issue, so it's up to states.

It's important to keep an eye on state legislation because sometimes proposed changes aren't positive, usually because the legislators are misinformed by an individual or organization with a personal agenda. Psychiatric Service Dog Partners (PSDP) does a good job of staying on top of potential issues like this, and you can do so as well by following along on their website (**www.psychdogpartners.org**).

Psychiatric service dogs are gaining acceptance across the country and around the world, but for most people it's still a large leap from wishing for a service dog to obtaining one. It sure would be nice if a psychiatrist could write you a prescription for a service dog and your health insurance company would help you obtain and pay for one just as they pay for other ongoing therapies and medications. We aren't there yet, but it's a nice vision for the future.

Thankfully, you're not restricted to waiting for someone else to figure out that you would benefit from a psychiatric service dog and provide one for you. If you think a service dog might be the change that restores quality of life you've lost to a mental health impairment, you have options. Take a serious look into what psychiatric service dogs can and can't do and the pros and cons of partnering with one of these amazing canines. These dogs aren't a magical cure for chronic mental illness, but they can trigger drastic improvements in quality of life for certain people. Maybe you or someone you love is one of them.

Appendixes

A: Federal FAQs

B: Sample Letters

C: Tips for Medical Professionals Writing a Service Dog or Emotional Support Animal Letter

D: Fundraising Tips

E: Glossary

Appendix A

Federal FAQs

Businesses and individuals can get lost in the maze of the Americans with Disabilities Act (ADA) and the regulations that implement it, even as they seek to comply. To help people find their way to compliance, the U.S. Department of Justice has created several publications that provide guidance to individuals and organizations:

- *ADA Revised Requirements: Service Animals-* This publication provides a summary of service animal provisions in the 2010 revision of the ADA.

- *Frequently Asked Questions about Service Animals and the ADA* - A collection of 37 questions and answers providing guidance on about ADA provisions for service animals.

- *Commonly Asked Questions About Service Animals in Places of Business* - This is an old FAQ you may still run across, but it's been replaced by Frequently Asked Questions about Service Animals and the ADA.

These documents translate sometimes vague-sounding regulations into specifics that are easy to understand and implement. The two which are still current are reproduced in their entirety in this appendix.

ADA Revised Requirements: Service Animals

Source: U.S. Department of Justice: Civil Rights Division: Disability Rights Section. ADA Revised Requirements: Service Animals. Washington, DC, 2011. Available from: **https://www.ada.gov/service_animals_2010.pdf**; Accessed: 10/30/2016.

The Department of Justice published revised final regulations implementing the Americans with Disabilities Act (ADA) for title II (State and local government services) and title III (public accommodations and commercial facilities) on September 15, 2010, in the Federal Register. These requirements, or rules, clarify and refine issues that have arisen over the past 20 years and contain new, and updated, requirements, including the 2010 Standards for Accessible Design (2010 Standards).

Overview

This publication provides guidance on the term "service animal" and the service animal provisions in the Department's new regulations.

- Beginning on March 15, 2011, only dogs are recognized as service animals under titles II and III of the ADA.

- A service animal is a dog that is individually trained to do work or perform tasks for a person with a disability.

- Generally, title II and title III entities must permit service animals to accompany people with disabilities in all areas where members of the public are allowed to go.

How "Service Animal" Is Defined

Service animals are defined as dogs that are individually trained to do work or perform tasks for people with disabilities. Examples of such work or tasks include guiding people who are blind, alerting people who are deaf, pulling a wheelchair, alerting and protecting a person who is having a seizure, reminding a person with mental illness to take prescribed medications, calming a person with Post Traumatic Stress

Disorder (PTSD) during an anxiety attack, or performing other duties. Service animals are working animals, not pets. The work or task a dog has been trained to provide must be directly related to the person's disability. Dogs whose sole function is to provide comfort or emotional support do not qualify as service animals under the ADA.

This definition does not affect or limit the broader definition of "assistance animal" under the Fair Housing Act or the broader definition of "service animal" under the Air Carrier Access Act.

Some State and local laws also define service animal more broadly than the ADA does. Information about such laws can be obtained from the State attorney general's office.

Where Service Animals Are Allowed

Under the ADA, State and local governments, businesses, and nonprofit organizations that serve the public generally must allow service animals to accompany people with disabilities in all areas of the facility where the public is normally allowed to go. For example, in a hospital it would be inappropriate to exclude a service animal from areas such as patient rooms, clinics, cafeterias, or examination rooms. However, it may be appropriate to exclude a service animal from operating rooms or burn units where the animal's presence may compromise a sterile environment.

Service Animals Must Be Under Control

Under the ADA, service animals must be harnessed, leashed, or tethered, unless these devices interfere with the service animal's work or the individual's disability prevents using these devices. In that case, the individual must maintain control of the animal through voice, signal, or other effective controls.

Inquiries, Exclusions, Charges, and Other Specific Rules Related to Service Animals

- When it is not obvious what service an animal provides, only limited inquiries are allowed. Staff may ask two questions: (1) is the dog a service animal required because of a disability, and (2) what work or task has the dog been trained to perform. Staff cannot ask about the person's disability, require medical documentation, require a special identification card or training documentation for the dog, or ask that the dog demonstrate its ability to perform the work or task.

- Allergies and fear of dogs are not valid reasons for denying access or refusing service to people using service animals. When a person who is allergic to dog dander and a person who uses a service animal must spend time in the same room or facility, for example, in a school classroom or at a homeless shelter, they both should be accommodated by assigning them, if possible, to different locations within the room or different rooms in the facility.

- A person with a disability cannot be asked to remove his service animal from the premises unless: (1) the dog is out of control and the handler does not take effective action to control it or (2) the dog is not housebroken. When there is a legitimate reason to ask that a service animal be removed, staff must offer the person with the disability the opportunity to obtain goods or services without the animal's presence.

- Establishments that sell or prepare food must allow service animals in public areas even if state or local health codes prohibit animals on the premises.

- People with disabilities who use service animals cannot be isolated from other patrons, treated less favorably than other patrons, or charged fees that are not charged to other patrons without animals. In addition, if a business requires a deposit or fee to be paid by patrons with pets, it must waive the charge for service animals.

- If a business such as a hotel normally charges guests for damage that they cause, a customer with a disability may also be charged for damage caused by himself or his service animal.

- Staff are not required to provide care or food for a service animal.

Miniature Horses

In addition to the provisions about service dogs, the Department's revised ADA regulations have a new, separate provision about miniature horses that have been individually trained to do work or perform tasks for people with disabilities. (Miniature horses generally range in height from 24 inches to 34 inches measured to the shoulders and generally weigh between 70 and 100 pounds.) Entities covered by the ADA must modify their policies to permit miniature horses where reasonable. The regulations set out four assessment factors to assist entities in determining whether miniature horses can be accommodated in their facility. The assessment factors are (1) whether the miniature horse is housebroken; (2) whether the miniature horse is under the owner's control; (3) whether the facility can accommodate the miniature horse's type, size, and weight; and (4) whether the miniature horse's presence will not compromise legitimate safety requirements necessary for safe operation of the facility.

For more information about the ADA, please visit our website or call our toll-free number.

ADA Website

www.ADA.gov

To receive e-mail notifications when new ADA information is available, visit the ADA Website's home page and click the **link** near the top of the middle column.

ADA Information Line

800-514-0301 (Voice) and 800-514-0383 (TTY)
24 hours a day to order publications by mail.
M-W, F 9:30 a.m. – 5:30 p.m., Th 12:30 p.m. – 5:30 p.m. (Eastern Time)
to speak with an ADA Specialist. All calls are confidential.

For persons with disabilities, this publication is available in alternate formats.

Duplication of this document is encouraged. July 2011

Frequently Asked Questions about Service Animals and the ADA

Source: U.S. Department of Justice: Civil Rights Division: Disability Rights Section. *Frequently Asked Questions about Service Animals and the ADA*. Washington, DC, 2015. Available from: **https://www.ada.gov/regs2010/service_animal_qa.pdf**; Accessed: 10/30/2016.

Many people with disabilities use a service animal in order to fully participate in everyday life. Dogs can be trained to perform many important tasks to assist people with disabilities, such as providing stability for a person who has difficulty walking, picking up items for a person who uses a wheelchair, preventing a child with autism from wandering away, or alerting a person who has hearing loss when someone is approaching from behind.

The Department of Justice continues to receive many questions about how the Americans with Disabilities Act (ADA) applies to service animals. The ADA requires State and local government agencies, businesses, and nonprofit organizations (covered entities) that provide goods or services to the public to make "reasonable modifications" in their policies, practices, or procedures when necessary to accommodate people with disabilities. The service animal rules fall under this general principle. Accordingly, entities that have a "no pets" policy generally must modify the policy to allow service animals into their facilities. This publication provides guidance on the ADA's service animal provisions and should be read in conjunction with the publication **ADA Revised Requirements: Service Animals**.

DEFINITION OF A SERVICE ANIMAL

Q1. What is a service animal?

A. Under the ADA, a service animal is defined as a dog that has been individually trained to do work or perform tasks for an individual with a disability. The task(s) performed by the dog must be directly related to the person's disability.

Q2. What does "do work or perform tasks" mean?

A. The dog must be trained to take a specific action when needed to assist the person with a disability. For example, a person with diabetes may have a dog that is trained to alert him when his blood sugar reaches high or low levels. A person with depression may have a dog that is trained to remind her to take her medication. Or, a person who has epilepsy may have a dog that is trained to detect the onset of a seizure and then help the person remain safe during the seizure.

Q3. Are emotional support, therapy, comfort, or companion animals considered service animals under the ADA?

A. No. These terms are used to describe animals that provide comfort just by being with a person. Because they have not been trained to perform a specific job or task, they do not qualify as service animals under the ADA. However, some State or local governments have laws that allow people to take emotional support animals into public places. You may check with your State and local government agencies to find out about these laws.

Q4. If someone's dog calms them when having an anxiety attack, does this qualify it as a service animal?

A. It depends. The ADA makes a distinction between psychiatric service animals and emotional support animals. If the dog has been trained to sense that an anxiety attack is about to happen and take a specific action to help avoid the attack or lessen its impact, that would qualify as a service animal. However, if the dog's mere presence provides comfort, that would not be considered a service animal under the ADA.

Q5. Does the ADA require service animals to be professionally trained?

A. No. People with disabilities have the right to train the dog themselves and are not required to use a professional service dog training program.

Q6. Are service-animals-in-training considered service animals under the ADA?

A. No. Under the ADA, the dog must already be trained before it can be taken into public places. However, some State or local laws cover animals that are still in training.

GENERAL RULES

Q7. What questions can a covered entity's employees ask to determine if a dog is a service animal?

A. In situations where it is not obvious that the dog is a service animal, staff may ask only two specific questions: (1) is the dog a service animal required because of a disability? and (2) what work or task has the dog been trained to perform? Staff are not allowed to request any documentation for the dog, require that the dog demonstrate its task, or inquire about the nature of the person's disability.

Q8. Do service animals have to wear a vest or patch or special harness identifying them as service animals?

A. No. The ADA does not require service animals to wear a vest, ID tag, or specific harness.

Q9. Who is responsible for the care and supervision of a service animal?

A. The handler is responsible for caring for and supervising the service animal, which includes toileting, feeding, and grooming and veterinary care. Covered entities are not obligated to supervise or otherwise care for a service animal.

Q10. Can a person bring a service animal with them as they go through a salad bar or other self-service food lines?

A. Yes. Service animals must be allowed to accompany their handlers to and through self-service food lines. Similarly, service animals may not be prohibited from communal food preparation areas, such as are commonly found in shelters or dormitories.

Q11. Can hotels assign designated rooms for guests with service animals, out of consideration for other guests?

A. No. A guest with a disability who uses a service animal must be provided the same opportunity to reserve any available room at the hotel as other guests without disabilities. They may not be restricted to "pet-friendly" rooms.

Q12. Can hotels charge a cleaning fee for guests who have service animals?

No. Hotels are not permitted to charge guests for cleaning the hair or dander shed by a service animal. However, if a guest's service animal causes damages to a guest room, a hotel is permitted to charge the same fee for damages as charged to other guests.

Q13. Can people bring more than one service animal into a public place?

A. Generally, yes. Some people with disabilities may use more than one service animal to perform different tasks. For example, a person who has a visual disability and a seizure disorder may use one service animal to assist with way-finding and another that is trained as a seizure alert dog. Other people may need two service animals for the same task, such as a person who needs two dogs to assist him or her with stability when walking. Staff may ask the two permissible questions (See Question 7) about each of the dogs. If both dogs can be accommodated, both should be allowed in. In some circumstances, however, it may not be possible to accommodate more than one service animal. For example, in a crowded small restaurant, only one dog may be able to fit under the table. The only other place for the second dog would be in the aisle, which would block the space between tables. In this case, staff may request that one of the dogs be left outside.

Q14. Does a hospital have to allow an in-patient with a disability to keep a service animal in his or her room?

A. Generally, yes. Service animals must be allowed in patient rooms and anywhere else in the hospital the public and patients are allowed to go. They cannot be excluded on the grounds that staff can provide the same services.

Q15. What happens if a patient who uses a service animal is admitted to the hospital and is unable to care for or supervise their animal?

A. If the patient is not able to care for the service animal, the patient can make arrangements for a family member or friend to come to the hospital to provide these services, as it is always preferable that the service animal and its handler not be separated, or to keep the dog during the hospitalization. If the patient is unable to care for the dog and is unable to arrange for someone else to care for the dog, the hospital may place the dog in a boarding facility until the patient is released, or make other appropriate arrangements. However, the hospital must give the patient the opportunity to make arrangements for the dog's care before taking such steps.

Q16. Must a service animal be allowed to ride in an ambulance with its handler?

A. Generally, yes. However, if the space in the ambulance is crowded and the dog's presence would interfere with the emergency medical staff's ability to treat the patient, staff should make other arrangements to have the dog transported to the hospital.

CERTIFICATION AND REGISTRATION

Q17. Does the ADA require that service animals be certified as service animals?

A. No. Covered entities may not require documentation, such as proof that the animal has been certified, trained, or licensed as a service animal, as a condition for entry.

There are individuals and organizations that sell service animal certification or registration documents online. These documents do not convey any rights under the ADA and the Department of Justice does not recognize them as proof that the dog is a service animal.

Q18. My city requires all dogs to be vaccinated. Does this apply to my service animal?

A. Yes. Individuals who have service animals are not exempt from local animal control or public health requirements.

Q19. My city requires all dogs to be registered and licensed. Does this apply to my service animal?

A. Yes. Service animals are subject to local dog licensing and registration requirements.

Q20. My city requires me to register my dog as a service animal. Is this legal under the ADA?

A. No. Mandatory registration of service animals is not permissible under the ADA. However, as stated above, service animals are subject to the same licensing and vaccination rules that are applied to all dogs.

Q21. My city / college offers a voluntary registry program for people with disabilities who use service animals and provides a special tag identifying the dogs as service animals. Is this legal under the ADA?

A. Yes. Colleges and other entities, such as local governments, may offer voluntary registries. Many communities maintain a voluntary registry that serves a public purpose, for example, to ensure that emergency staff know to look for service animals during an emergency evacuation process. Some offer a benefit, such as a reduced dog license fee, for individuals who register their service animals. Registries for purposes like this are permitted under the ADA. An entity may not, however, require that a dog be registered as a service animal as a condition of being permitted in public places. This would be a violation of the ADA.

BREEDS

Q22. Can service animals be any breed of dog?

A. Yes. The ADA does not restrict the type of dog breeds that can be service animals.

Q23. Can individuals with disabilities be refused access to a facility based solely on the breed of their service animal?

A. No. A service animal may not be excluded based on assumptions or stereotypes about the animal's breed or how the animal might behave. However, if a particular service animal behaves in a way that poses a direct threat to the health or safety of others, has a history of such behavior, or is not under the control of the handler, that animal may be excluded. If an animal is excluded for such reasons, staff must still offer their goods or services to the person without the animal present.

Q24. If a municipality has an ordinance that bans certain dog breeds, does the ban apply to service animals?

A. No. Municipalities that prohibit specific breeds of dogs must make an exception for a service animal of a prohibited breed, unless the dog poses a direct threat to the health or safety of others. Under the "direct threat" provisions of the ADA, local jurisdictions need to determine, on a case-by-case basis, whether a particular service animal can be excluded based on that particular animal's actual behavior or history, but they may not exclude a service animal because of fears or generalizations about how an animal or breed might behave. It is important to note that breed restrictions differ significantly from jurisdiction to jurisdiction. In fact, some jurisdictions have no breed restrictions.

EXCLUSION OF SERVICE ANIMALS

Q25. When can service animals be excluded?

A. The ADA does not require covered entities to modify policies, practices, or procedures if it would "fundamentally alter" the nature of the goods, services, programs, or activities provided to the public. Nor does it overrule legitimate safety requirements. If admitting service animals would fundamentally alter the nature of a service or program, service animals may be prohibited. In addition, if a particular service animal is out of control and the handler does not take effective action to control it, or if it is not housebroken, that animal may be excluded.

Q26. When might a service dog's presence fundamentally alter the nature of a service or program provided to the public?

A. In most settings, the presence of a service animal will not result in a fundamental alteration. However, there are some exceptions. For example, at a boarding school, service animals could be restricted from a specific area of a dormitory reserved specifically for students with allergies to dog dander. At a zoo, service animals can be restricted from areas where the animals on display are the natural prey or natural predators of dogs, where the presence of a dog would be disruptive, causing the displayed animals to behave aggressively or become agitated. They cannot be restricted from other areas of the zoo.

Q27. What does under control mean? Do service animals have to be on a leash? Do they have to be quiet and not bark?

A. The ADA requires that service animals be under the control of the handler at all times. In most instances, the handler will be the individual with a disability or a third party who accompanies the individual with a disability. In the school (K-12) context and in similar settings, the school or similar entity may need to provide some assistance to enable a particular student to handle his or her service animal. The service animal must be harnessed, leashed, or tethered while in public places unless these devices interfere with the service animal's work or the person's disability prevents use of these devices. In that case, the person must use voice, signal, or other effective means to maintain control of the animal. For example, a person who uses a wheelchair may use a long, retractable leash to allow her service animal to pick up or retrieve items. She may not allow the dog to wander away from her and must maintain control of the dog, even if it is retrieving an item at a distance from her. Or, a returning veteran who has PTSD and has great difficulty entering unfamiliar spaces may have a dog that is trained to enter a space, check to see that no threats are there, and come back and signal that it is safe to enter. The dog must be off leash to do its job, but may be leashed at other times. Under control also means that a service animal should not be allowed to bark repeatedly in a lecture hall, theater, library, or other quiet place. However, if a dog barks just once, or barks because someone has provoked it, this would not mean that the dog is out of control.

Q28. What can my staff do when a service animal is being disruptive?

A. If a service animal is out of control and the handler does not take effective action to control it, staff may request that the animal be removed from the premises.

Q29. Are hotel guests allowed to leave their service animals in their hotel room when they leave the hotel?

A. No, the dog must be under the handler's control at all times.

Q30. What happens if a person thinks a covered entity's staff has discriminated against him or her?

A. Individuals who believe that they have been illegally denied access or service because they use service animals may file a complaint with the U.S. Department of Justice. Individuals also have the right to file a private lawsuit in Federal court charging the entity with discrimination under the ADA.

MISCELLANEOUS

Q31. Are stores required to allow service animals to be placed in a shopping cart?

A. Generally, the dog must stay on the floor, or the person must carry the dog. For example, if a person with diabetes has a glucose alert dog, he may carry the dog in a chest pack so it can be close to his face to allow the dog to smell his breath to alert him of a change in glucose levels.

Q32. Are restaurants, bars, and other places that serve food or drink required to allow service animals to be seated on chairs or allow the animal to be fed at the table?

A. No. Seating, food, and drink are provided for customer use only. The ADA gives a person with a disability the right to be accompanied by his or her service animal, but covered entities are not required to allow an animal to sit or be fed at the table.

Q33. Are gyms, fitness centers, hotels, or municipalities that have swimming pools required to allow a service animal in the pool with its handler?

A. No. The ADA does not override public health rules that prohibit dogs in swimming pools. However, service animals must be allowed on the pool deck and in other areas where the public is allowed to go.

Q34. Are churches, temples, synagogues, mosques, and other places of worship required to allow individuals to bring their service animals into the facility?

A. No. Religious institutions and organizations are specifically exempt from the ADA. However, there may be State laws that apply to religious organizations.

Q35. Do apartments, mobile home parks, and other residential properties have to comply with the ADA?

A. The ADA applies to housing programs administered by state and local governments, such as public housing authorities, and by places of public accommodation, such as public and private universities. In addition, the Fair Housing Act applies to virtually all types of housing, both public and privately-owned, including housing covered by the ADA. Under the Fair Housing Act, housing providers are obligated to permit, as a reasonable accommodation, the use of animals that work, provide assistance, or perform tasks that benefit persons with a disabilities, or provide emotional support to alleviate a symptom or effect of a disability. For information about these Fair Housing Act requirements see HUD's **Notice on Service Animals and Assistance Animals for People with Disabilities in Housing and HUD-funded Programs**.

Q36. Do Federal agencies, such as the U.S. Department of Veterans Affairs, have to comply with the ADA?

A. No. Section 504 of the Rehabilitation Act of 1973 is the Federal law that protects the rights of people with disabilities to participate in Federal programs and services. For information or to file a complaint, contact the agency's equal opportunity office.

Q37. Do commercial airlines have to comply with the ADA?

A. No. The Air Carrier Access Act is the Federal law that protects the rights of people with disabilities in air travel. For information or to file a complaint, contact the U.S. Department of Transportation, Aviation Consumer Protection Division, at 202-366-2220.

RESOURCES

For more information about the ADA, please visit our website or call our toll-free number.

ADA WEBSITE

www.ADA.gov

To receive e-mail notifications when new ADA information is available, visit the ADA Website's home page and click the link near the bottom of the right-hand column.

ADA INFORMATION LINE

800-514-0301 (Voice) and 800-514-0383 (TTY) M-W, F 9:30 a.m. – 5:30 p.m., Th 12:30 p.m. – 5:30 p.m. (Eastern Time) to speak with an ADA Specialist. Calls are confidential. For people with disabilities, this publication is available in alternate formats.

Duplication of this document is encouraged.
July 2015

Appendix B

Sample Letters

You don't need a letter to have a service dog, but you may need one for a specific purpose, such as flying with a psychiatric service dog, living in no-pets housing, or supporting a reasonable accommodation request at work. A doctor's letter doesn't turn a dog into a service dog, but when you do have a service dog or service dog in training, letters can help you secure accommodations you need.

The examples in this section demonstrate what different types of letters might include. There's no such thing as a one-size-fits-all letter, so you will need to adapt and customize each one to meet your needs. If you're not sure which letter applies when, review Chapter 6: Knowing Service Dog Laws. Please remember that these letters are intended as a guide only and aren't legal advice. For a list of tips for medical professionals to consider when writing support letters, see Appendix C.

PSD Housing Accommodation Request Letter from a Person with a Disability

Your Name
Your Address

Date

Jane Doe, Housing Manager
123 Main Street
Somewhere, NC

Dear Ms. Doe,

I am a tenant of 123 Main Street, apartment #1. I am writing to request a reasonable accommodation under the federal Fair Housing Act to allow my service dog to reside with me despite the "no pets" policy. I have a psychiatric disability that impedes my ability to live independently. I require the assistance of my service dog to mitigate the functional limitations created by my disability.

A letter from my medical provider is attached, providing verification of my disability, functional limitations, and my need for a service dog. My service dog performs tasks that greatly benefit my daily life, including **[task list],** and is necessary for my well-being.

Thank you for your consideration. I look forward to your prompt reply.

Sincerely,

Signature: _____ Date: _____

SDiT Housing Accommodation Request Letter from a Person with a Disability

Your Name
Your Address

Date

Jane Doe, Housing Manager
123 Main Street
Somewhere, NC

Dear Ms. Doe,

I am a tenant of 123 Main Street, apartment #1. I have a psychiatric disability that impedes my ability to live independently. I am in the process of training a service dog to mitigate the functional limitations created by my disability. I am writing to request a reasonable accommodation under the federal Fair Housing Act to allow my service dog in training to reside with me despite your "no pets" policy.

A letter from my medical provider is attached, providing verification of my disability, functional limitations, and my need for a service dog. My dog will be trained to perform tasks that greatly benefit my daily life, including **[task list],** and is necessary for my well-being.

Thank you for your consideration. I look forward to your prompt reply.

Sincerely,

Signature: _____ Date: _____

PSD Housing Accommodation Request Letter from a Medical Provider

[Print on provider's letterhead]

Date

To Whom It May Concern:

[Full name] is my patient and is under my care. **[He/She]** meets the definition for disability under the Americans with Disabilities Act, the Fair Housing Act, and the Rehabilitation Act of 1973.

[His/Her] disability causes certain functional limitations. These limitations include **[list limitations].**

In order to help alleviate these difficulties and to enhance **[his/her]** ability to live independently and to fully use and enjoy the dwelling unit you own and/or administer, **[he/she]** requires the assistance of **[his/her]** service dog. The presence of this assistance animal is necessary for **[his/her]** health because it is individually trained to perform tasks that help mitigate **[his/her]** disability.

Thank you for providing this reasonable accommodation for my patient.

Sincerely,

Signature: _____ Date: _____

SDiT/ESA Housing Accommodation Request Letter from a Medical Provider

[Print on provider's letterhead]

Date

To Whom It May Concern:

[Full name] is my patient and is under my care. **[He/She]** meets the definition for disability under the Americans with Disabilities Act, the Fair Housing Act, and the Rehabilitation Act of 1973.

[His/Her] disability causes certain functional limitations. These limitations include **[list limitations].**

In order to help alleviate these difficulties and to enhance **[his/her]** ability to live independently and to fully use and enjoy the dwelling unit you own and/or administer, **[he/she]** requires the assistance of **[his/her]** emotional support dog. The presence of this assistance animal is necessary for **[his/her]** health.

Thank you for providing this reasonable accommodation for my patient.

Sincerely,

Signature: _____ Date: _____

PSD Flying Letter from a Medical Provider

[Print on provider's letterhead]

Date

To Whom It May Concern:

I am currently treating **[full name]** for a mental health or emotional disability recognized in the Diagnostic and Statistical Manual of Mental Disorders (DSM-V). This person needs **[his/her]** dog to travel as a psychiatric service animal for air travel and/or for activity at the destination. My **[type of license]** was issued in the state or jurisdiction of **[location]** in **[year].**

Signature: _____ Date: _____

ESA Flying Letter from a Medical Provider

[Print on provider's letterhead]

Date

To Whom It May Concern:

I am currently treating **[full name]** for a mental health or emotional disability recognized in the Diagnostic and Statistical Manual of Mental Disorders (DSM-V). This person needs **[his/her]** dog to travel as an emotional support animal for air travel and/or for activity at the destination. My **[type of license]** was issued in the state or jurisdiction of **[location]** in **[year].**

Signature: _____ Date: _____

PSD Workplace Accommodation Request from a Person with a Disability

Your Name
Your Address

Date

Jane Doe, Manager
Your Company
123 Main Street
Somewhere, NC

Dear Ms. Doe,

I am writing to request a reasonable accommodation under the Americans with Disabilities Act **[Rehabilitation Act of 1973 if you are a federal employee]**. I have a disability that impedes my ability to perform certain job functions, including **[list tasks]**. To alleviate these difficulties and allow me to perform my job and fully participate in the workplace, I request that you to allow my trained service dog to accompany me at work. My service dog performs tasks that enable me to perform my work, including **[task list],** and is necessary for my well-being.

A letter from my medical provider is attached, providing verification of my disability, functional limitations, and need for a service dog.

Thank you for your consideration. I look forward to your reply.

Sincerely,

Signature: _____ Date: _____

PSD Workplace Accommodation Request Letter from a Medical Provider

[Print on provider's letterhead]

To Whom It May Concern:

[Full name] is my patient and is under my care. **[He/She]** meets the definition for disability under the Americans with Disabilities Act and the Rehabilitation Act of 1973.

[His/Her] disability causes certain functional limitations. These limitations include **[list limitations]**.

In order to help alleviate these difficulties and to enable **[him/her]** to perform **[his/her]** job and fully participate in the workplace, **[he/she]** requires the assistance of **[his/her]** service dog. The presence of this assistance animal is necessary for **[his/her]** workplace functioning because it is individually trained to perform tasks that help mitigate **[his/her]** disability. Please allow **[his/her]** service dog to accompany **[him/her]** in the workplace.

Thank you for providing this reasonable accommodation for my patient.

Sincerely,

Signature: _____ Date: _____

Appendix C

Writing a Letter for a Service Dog or Emotional Support Animal: Tips for Medical Professionals

When writing a letter supporting a patient's need for a service dog or emotional support animal, there are several key things to keep in mind:

Know the differences between a service dog and an emotional support animal and use the appropriate term in your letter. A service dog is individually trained to perform tasks that specifically mitigate the symptoms of a person's disability. An emotional support animal provides comfort and support for a person with a disability but may not have any special training (or even be a dog).

Does your patient's condition rise to the level of a disability? A diagnosis does not automatically equal a disability. A disability is an impairment that substantially interferes with the patient's ability to carry out functions of daily life. To qualify for a service animal or an emotional support animal, the patient's condition must rise to the level of disability.

Identify the purpose of the letter. A person doesn't need a letter from a physician to have a service dog. However, documentation can be required for some purposes, such as air travel, living in "no-pets" housing, or obtaining a reasonable accommodation to bring a service dog to work under the

Americans with Disabilities Act (ADA). A patient who is applying to a service dog organization to receive a service dog may also need a supporting letter. Your letter should assess the benefits a service or assistance dog provides to your patient. You're not required to evaluate the training of a particular dog.

Identify and include the necessary elements. These will vary slightly depending on purpose, but letters always need to include these four things:

1) The person's full name and that they are under your care.

2) Confirmation that the person has a mental health diagnosis and meets the definition of disability. For most purposes you don't have to specifically name the diagnosis(es), although for flying you must mention that it's a diagnosis included in the DSM.

3) Confirmation that the service dog or emotional support animal is needed to help mitigate the disability. For housing and work accommodation requests, be specific about the work or tasks the dog performs to aid the patient, but that's not necessary in letters related to flying.

4) Your professional credentials.

The letter should be printed on your office letterhead, signed, and dated. From time to time the patient may need a new or updated letter.

For additional detailed advice on writing these letters, see: John J. Ensminger LLM & J. Lawrence Thomas PhD (2013) *Writing Letters to Help Patients with Service and Support Animals*, Journal of Forensic Psychology Practice, 13:2, 92-115, DOI: 10.1080/15228932.2013.765734

Appendix D

Fundraising Tips

Cost is a big concern when considering partnering with a service dog. The gap between desiring a psychiatric service dog and being able to afford one can be overwhelming. Friends and family may be willing to help but often can't offer as much you'll need. It's a common situation, and many would-be handlers tackle it by undertaking a variety of fundraising efforts. By taking a multi-pronged approach, they're able to come up with a significant chunk of the necessary finances.

When attempting to raise a large sum of money, it's easy to get lost in the magnitude of the sum. However, in many ways it's a lot like writing a book, as it can be accomplished in increments that can range in size from tiny to substantial, yet all add progress toward the final goal. This book wasn't written in a week or a month or even steadily over time; it was written in pieces incrementally; some weeks only a few pages were accomplished, others an entire chapter flowed forth. Eventually, as you can tell, the project was completed, and the book was published. Fundraising for a service dog tends to take a similar course, full of little bits and pieces that add up to eventually form the whole. Try to remember that it's a process, and don't get discouraged if it takes a long time to reach your goal. Just keep striving, and you'll eventually get there.

Online fundraising tools make it easier than ever for you to raise money for a service dog, but don't overlook direct, "offline" requests, which can bring in as much or more and tend to be a bit more private.

Speaking of privacy, one thing you need to decide up front is how much of it you're willing to give up in pursuit your fundraising goals. Full on, public fundraising efforts bring the highest success rates but aren't for everyone. Online fundraising is a very public process. To have any chance at success, you'll have to disclose personal details about yourself and why you need a service dog. You'll need to post photos and/or videos of yourself. Anybody, including your co-workers, mother-in-law, and the neighbours across the street may come to know that you have disabling mental health issues and that you also need financial help. You'll have to give enough detail to convince people that you are genuinely deserving of their financial assistance even though they may not personally know you. This is not a road everyone feels comfortable taking, so consider carefully if your personality is suited for it. If you can't drive down it whole-heartedly, your chances for success are more limited and certainly it will take longer to reach your goal.

When asking for help paying for a service dog, people who are obtaining a dog from a service dog program tend to have a substantial advantage. Donors are more willing to write checks to a recognized service dog organization on your behalf rather than write them directly to you. It provides a sense of reassurance that the donation will go toward its intended purpose. In addition, if the program is a registered 501(c)(3) charity, every contribution is a potential tax deduction for the donor. You can still fundraise for an owner-trained service dog, but it's likely to be more difficult, and you'll need to do everything possible to assure donors exactly how their contribution will be spent.

Setting Goals and Keeping Records

Before you start asking for contributions, you'll need to figure out how much money you need to raise and for what purposes. For this you're going to have to buckle down and create a service dog budget. It won't be easy because the costs aren't set in stone and can vary substantially.

If you've been accepted by a program, they can help you create a budget and in some cases even give you some fundraising advice. Remember to factor in travel expenses if you'll need to go to the program's offices for team training and to fetch your dog. In such cases your budget might look something like this:

```
$15,000  Program fee
    $600  Air tickets for self and companion to team training
  $1,000  Lodging and food during team training
------------
$16,600  Total to fundraise
```

If you're planning to train your own service dog, your budget will need to include the cost of obtaining a candidate and professional training fees. Owner training budgets are very individual. Here are a few examples:

Example 1:

```
  $100 Candidate pre-adoption assessment by a professional trainer
   $70 Rescue adoption fee
  $100 Puppy group obedience classes
$2,000 Private training lessons
----------
$2,270  Total to fundraise
```

Example 2:

```
$2,000 Started dog from breeder
$2,500 Board & train session at K9 Genius Services
$2,000 Private training lessons
----------
$7,000  Total to fundraise
```

You might think that there are a few things missing from these budgets. What about food and veterinary care? Those aren't included because they aren't things you should need to fundraise to achieve. This fundraising advice is meant for large, distinct expenses. If you can't afford the ongoing expenses of owning and caring for your dog, then you should wait until you can before obtaining one. Everyday needs like food and heartworm prevention can't be left hanging, waiting to see if you get donations to cover them or not.

Once you know your ultimate fundraising goal, set mini-goals. These will help you recognize the progress you're making and help you stay on track. Your first goal might simply be to raise $100. Then perhaps your next goal might be to raise the initial cost of your candidate dog. Milestones don't have to exactly match your budget line items, but it's important to have them.

Set up a place to track progress toward your goals. An inexpensive notebook will work, as will a spreadsheet. Choose whatever format you prefer, but tracking is a must. You should always know how much you have received and from whom.

Always thank givers, no matter how small the donation. Thank them immediately, and then thank them again when you reach your goal. Include a picture of yourself and your service dog/prospect. If someone says no, pay attention to the reason; you may be able to use it to help improve your pitch.

Asking for Donations

Start by asking people you know. Asking directly is the best approach, but if you use social media sites such as Facebook, you can also post an appeal there and ask people to share it. Keep an eye out for business and organizations that regularly donate things. Who supports the local sports teams, charitable groups, and similar efforts? You can discover donor candidates from information printed on items such as menus and t-shirts or listed in newspaper articles.

Set up a page on an online fundraising site such as YouCaring (**www.youcaring.com**) or GoFundMe (**www.gofundme.com**). Rather than setting up multiple accounts across these sites, pick your favorite and make it shine. Your page should state very specifically how the funds will be used and include a fundraising goal. Setting a $10,000 goal so that you can pay for a service dog from a specific program that you've already been accepted to is going to go over better with donors than asking for the same amount "so I can acquire and train a service dog." That doesn't mean you can't raise money for an owner-trained service dog, but it does mean you need to be very specific about how the money will be used. When making your appeal, mention how much will be paid to whom and for what purposes. For example: $1000 for a qualified puppy from Fido Breeders, $5000 for professional training from Rover Dog Training School.

When building your page, look over other fundraising pages on the same platform and try to identify what the most successful fundraisers are doing. Do they perhaps have a video with a personal appeal? How much personal detail do they go into? Try to identify what's working for others and emulate it.

Once your fundraising page is live, ask friends or family to go there first. Ideally this will mean your page will already have some donations on it when you start sending people there and they won't be looking at a glaring zero dollars raised. Consider seeding the account with a contribution of your own, perhaps anonymously (or not).

Online fundraising is a great way to raise money, but it's not the only way. Contact local churches and community charitable organizations and tell them your story. Find out who is the pastor or leader of the congregation or organization and write them a personal letter. Your letter should explain why you need a service dog and ask if they have any funds available. They might ask for evidence to ensure your authenticity, such as a letter from the service dog program or from your doctor. It's possible they might hold a fundraiser such as a bake sale to help you out. You're greatest chances of success will be with local groups that pride themselves on serving the local community.

Participating in Give-Back Programs

Look for businesses that offer joint opportunities, where a portion of the proceeds for an event will be donated for a charitable purpose (such as your service dog). Many restaurant chains do this, including big names like Panera, Chipotle, and Wendy's restaurants. It's important to pay attention to the details of these deals. Some restaurants will give a percentage of the night's proceeds, while others will require you to hand out flyers and pay a percentage based on the flyers that are turned in. To find establishments near you, use a search engine and look for "restaurant give back nights."

Non-food businesses are often willing to do some form of this as well. Painting with a Twist, where attendees receive step-by-step art instruction and leave with a finished piece they created, periodically holds events (dubbed Painting with a Purpose) that are geared toward raising funds that stay in each franchisee's local market.

Another option is to ask local businesses if you can put a collection jar by their register, where customers can donate their change.

Getting Crafty and/or Clever

Straight donations aren't the only way to raise money, though perhaps they are the fastest. Look around you for things you can sell, whether you make them yourself and sell them in your own online store or piggyback on an online marketing platform. Several people have launched stores on Etsy and sell handmade crafts such as dog collars and leads. Another handler collects and shells pecans that fall from the trees in her front yard and sells them online. Things like these aren't going to have you rolling in the dough but you can do them yourself and they all add up and move you forward toward your ultimate goal.

If you're not particularly crafty but you are clever, you can hook into programs that let you add your creativity to their products and share the resulting profits with you. They take care of the ordering, payment processing, and shipping. You take care of the creativity and most of the promotion. Examples include:

- ✓ **T-shirt sales:** Create a clever t-shirt and sell it through Bonfire (**www.bonfire.com**), inkd apparel (**www.inkdapparel.com/fundraising/**) or a similar site.

- ✓ **Support bracelets:** Create jewelry designed around a theme. Bravelets, for example, are designed along the theme "Be Brave." Items are displayed on the Bravelets website (**www.bravelets.com**) and a percentage of each sale goes to you.

If you decide to fundraise for your service dog, bring your ingenuity and determination to the table. You will encounter the word no, but that's okay, just move on. It's normal, and you have

to be willing to push through it to reach your goal of having a
service dog at your side.

Glossary

access challenge: Someone questioning your right to bring your service dog into their establishment.

ADA: See Americans with Disabilities Act.

ADAAA: See Americans with Disabilities Act Amendments Act.

ADI: See Assistance Dogs International.

Air Carrier Access Act: A U.S. law that requires airlines to permit service animals and emotional support animals to travel in the cabin of commercial airlines with their disabled owner.

Americans with Disabilities Act (ADA): Federal legislation that prohibits discrimination against people with disabilities. The ADA became law in 1990.

Americans with Disabilities Act Amendments Act (ADAA): Federal legislation updating the Americans with Disabilities Act with new wording and provisions, including a revised definition of disability. The ADAAA was signed into law in 2008 and became effective on January 1, 2009.

assistance dog: A generic term for a dog trained to perform hearing, guide, mobility, psychiatric, or other work or tasks to aid a person with a disability. The Fair Housing Act has a slightly different definition that adds in animals which only provide emotional support.

Assistance Dogs International (ADI): An industry membership organization for nonprofit assistance dog organizations around the world.

blocking (task): Using its body as a barrier, the dog creates a zone of space between its handler nearby people.

breed specific legislation (BSL): Laws that apply special rules or ownership restrictions to dogs of particular breeds, such as pit bulls.

BSL: See breed-specific legislation.

candidate: A dog that's being considered for selection to begin training as a service dog. Similar to prospect.

Canine Good Citizen (CGC): An American Kennel Club (AKC) program that promotes responsible pet ownership and good manners for dogs. The CGC test is a 10-point assessment of foundational obedience skills. Dogs who formally pass this test may receive a certificate from the AKC.

counter-balance (task): Serving as a point of balance and stability for the handler to prevent falls and increase mobility. Service dogs wear special harnesses for this type of work.

CGC: See Canine Good Citizen test.

deep pressure therapy (DPT): A task where the dog applies its bodyweight to its handler in a specific way, such as lying atop the handler's chest and abdomen, in order to alleviate undesirable symptoms.

Department of Justice (DOJ): A department of the U.S. government charged with the enforcement of federal laws and administration of justice in the U.S. The DOJ enforces the Americans with Disabilities Act.

disability: A physical or mental impairment that substantially limits one or more major life activities of an individual.

DOJ: See Department of Justice.

DPT: See deep pressure therapy.

DSM-IV, DSM-V: Versions four and five of the Diagnostic and Statistical Manual of Mental Disorders, a manual published by the American Psychiatric Association that lists all classifications of mental disorders.

EEOC: See Equal Employment Opportunity Commission.

emotional support animal (ESA): An animal that provides emotional support and comfort to a person with a disability. No special training is required.

Equal Employment Opportunity Commission (EEOC): An agency of the federal government charged with interpreting and enforcing federal laws prohibiting discrimination.

ESA: See emotional support animal.

Fair Housing Act (FHAct): A U.S. law that requires housing providers covered by the act to provide "reasonable accommodations" to individuals with disabilities.

FHA: Federal Housing Administration. See also Fair Housing Act (FHAct).

grounding (task): Bringing oneself back to the "here and now" through deliberately reorienting mental focus to something specific in the present. It's used to help manage overwhelming feelings, anxiety, or dissociation, among other unpleasant sensations.

IAADP: See International Association of Assistance Dog Partners.

IDEA: See Individuals with Disabilities Education Act.

IEP: See Individualized Education Program.

Individualized Education Program (IEP): A document that identifies a child's learning needs, the services the school will provide, and how progress will be measured. The IDEA requires public schools to create an IEP for each child receiving special education services. An IEP may include permitting the student to be accompanied by a service dog.

Individuals with Disabilities Education Act (IDEA): Federal legislation enacted in 1975 to ensure that children with disabilities have equal access to a free appropriate public education (FAPE).

234 \ Saved by the Dog

intelligent disobedience: Willful refusal of a command because carrying it out would be unsafe or undesirable. Guide dogs are trained to ignore a command to move forward if it would take their handler into the path an oncoming car.

International Association of Assistance Dog Partners (IAADP): A nonprofit membership organization created in 1993 to serve the needs of individuals partnered with a service dog of any type, whether for physical or psychiatric disabilities.

light guide work: Guiding tasks aid people who need help navigating from point A to point B. Psychiatric service dogs are sometimes cross-trained in "light guide work," which means they can do things like guide the handler to a particular person or place if they are disoriented or perform momentum pulling to help a handler keep moving forward when dazed or confused.

light mobility: Mobility tasks aid people who have physical impairments that affect their ability to move around in the world. Psychiatric service dogs are sometime cross-trained in "light mobility," which means they provide minor mobility assistance such as retrieving dropped items, performing momentum pulling, or closing doors.

major life activity: Under the Americans with Disabilities Act (ADA), major life activities include, but are not limited to, caring for oneself, performing manual tasks, seeing, hearing, eating, sleeping, walking, standing, lifting, bending, speaking, breathing, learning, reading, concentrating, thinking, communicating, and working. Operation of major bodily functions, including but not limited to, functions of the immune system, normal cell growth, digestive, bowel, bladder, neurological, brain, respiratory, circulatory, endocrine, and reproductive functions, are also included.

medical alert dog: A dog trained to alert its handler to an impending medical event that the handler is unaware of, allowing the handler to take preventative or protective measures.

medical response dog: A dog trained to respond to a medical event in progress, such as a panic attack or a seizure that has already occurred.

momentum pull (task): Pulling the handler forward in the direction they are walking. This is helpful for people who are feeling weak or disoriented.

PAT: See public access test.

proofing: Practicing trained behavior in a variety of settings with increasing levels of distraction.

prospect: A dog that's being considered for selection to begin training as a service dog. Similar to candidate.

PSD: See psychiatric service dog.

PSDiT: See psychiatric service dog in training.

PSDP: See Psychiatric Service Dog Partners.

psychiatric service dog: A dog that is specially trained to assist an individual who has a mental health disability.

psychiatric service dog in training: A dog that is actively training to become a service dog for an individual who has a mental health disability.

Psychiatric Service Dog Partners (PSDP): A peer guidance and advocacy organization for the psychiatric service dog community. This organization was formed in 2012 and achieved 501(c) (3) charitable organization status in 2015.

public access test (PAT): A formal test that assesses a dog's readiness for regular outings to public settings.

reasonable accommodation: A change to a job, work, or housing environment so that an individual who has a disability can function in that setting as successfully as a non-disabled person.

Rehabilitation Act of 1973 (The Rehab Act): A precursor to the Americans with Disabilities Act (ADA) that's still in effect and covers some situations that the ADA doesn't. Commonly referred to as Section 504.

religious entity: A religious organization, including a place of worship. Religious entities are exempt from the ADA.

SDiT: See service dog in training.

Section 504: A section of The Rehabilitation Act of 1973, a precursor to the Americans with Disabilities Act (ADA) that's still in effect and covers some situations that the ADA doesn't.

service dog: A dog that is individually trained to help a person who has a disability.

service dog in training (SDiT): A dog that is actively training to become a service dog for a person with a disability.

task shopping: Seeking out tasks you can train your dog to do so that you can call it a service dog rather than identifying them based on your own symptoms and needs.

therapy dog: A dog that provides affection and comfort to people other than its owner. Therapy dogs often go with their owners on a volunteer basis to settings such as hospitals, retirement homes, and schools.

task (vs work): A trained assistive behavior that a service dog performs when given a cue, such as a verbal command or a hand signal.

TTY: A device used for telephone communication by people who are deaf or hard of hearing or speech impaired. A TTY device is required at both ends of the conversation. It allows users to converse by typing messages.

whale eye: A body language signal where the dog shows the whites of its eyes, often a sign of fear or aggression.

work (vs task): Trained behavior a dog is "on-call" to do as needed, without it being specifically requested. For example, a service dog may be trained to observe if their handler starts showing a particular sign of stress, such as clenched fists, and respond by pawing the handler's leg. The dog might need to do this anytime, anywhere and is not specifically requested to do so.

Index

access challenge, 44, 115, 154–57, 231

ADA Information Line, 140

ADA Revised Requirements: Service Animals, 194

advocacy, 158

aggression, warning signs, 82

Air Carrier Access Act, 231

Air Carrier Access Act (ACAA), 12, 124–26, 166, 209

airport potty facilities, 167

airport security, 168

AKC Canine Good Citizen (CGC), 83, 89

AKC Community Canine, 84

AKC Urban CGC (CGCU), 84

alerting (task), 27, 28

allergies, 117, 196

ambulances, 175, 203

American Temperament Test Society (ATTS) test, 78

Americans with Disabilities Act, 231

Americans with Disabilities Act (ADA), 4, 7, 82, 110–17
  definition of disability, 8–9, 111–13
  definition of service dog, 10, 114, 195
  exclusions, 112, 116
  Information Line, 140

public access rights, 114–17
  questions that can legally be asked, 115, 195, 201
  questions, answering, 148
  service dog in trainin, 201
  service dog in training, 114, 142
  Titles, 111

Americans with Disabilities Amendments Act, 231

amusement parks, 180

Animal Legal & Historical Center, 120, 140

Animal Planet Dog Breed Selector, 75

application process, 54–55

application, pre-screening, 53

ASPCA SAFER, 79

assistance animal, 121, 122, 124, 131, 140, 195, 208, 214, 215, 219

assistance dog, 231

Assistance Dogs International (ADI), 50, 92, 138, 231

Auburn University, 184

automobile travel, 170

benefits of pet ownership, 4

Berns, Gregory, 184

Bingo, 159

blocking (task), 31, 187, 231

Blogger, 135

blogs, 135

board & train, 104

breed selection, 75, 204

breed specific legislation (BSL), 73, 205, 232

Brown Aptitude Test for Service (BATS), 79–81

busses, 169

campgrounds, 178

Canine Companions for Independence (CCI), 185

Canine Good Citizen (CGC), 232

canine hip dysplasia (CHD), 75

capturing, 99

certification. See registration

Certification Council for Professional Dog Trainers, 100

church, 178, 208

clicker training, 99

commitment required, 15, 26, 56, 65

contract, professional training, 101

correction, 99

cortisol, 186

cost, 14, 26

counter-balance (task), 232

cover (task), 31

CPDT-KA, 100

cue, 99

deep pressure therapy (DPT), 29, 31, 32, 34, 35, 36, 232

dental appointments, 174

Department of Justice (DOJ), 111, 194, 199, 232

Diagnostic and Statistical Manual of Mental Disorders (DSM), 39, 124, 125, 232

dining out, 176, 196, 201

disability, definition of, 8–9, 232

Disney World, 180

distraction, 27, 36

doctor appointments, 173

documentation, 116, 117

documentation, 109

dog trainer. See professional trainer

DogTime Dog Matchup, 74

DPT. See deep pressure therapy (DPT)

Duke Canine Cognition Center of Duke University, The, 185

elevators, 163

emergency plan, 175

emergency rooms, 174

Emory University, 184

emotional support animal (ESA), 12, 27, 120, 124, 126, 200, 233

employment. See workplace environment

Equal Employment Opportunity Commission (EEOC), 111, 112, 118, 233

escalators, 162

etiquette, 144

Facebook groups, 51, 132–34

facilitated service dog teams, 38

Fair Housing Act (FHAct), 12, 120, 233

fake service dogs, 5, 159, 188

FAQs, 194, 199

FIDO, 186

FIDOS, 184

flying, 124–26
   airport potty facilities, 167
   airport security, 168
   how to, 169
   letter, 125, 216
   service dog in training, 126

focus, 153

Frequently Asked Questions about Service Animals and the ADA, 199

functional MRI, 184

Georgia Institute of Technology, 186

graduating, 63, 92

grounding (task), 29, 31, 32, 33, 34, 36, 233

group classes, 103

gym, 178

hospitals, 174, 202

hotels, 172–73, 196, 201

housing accommodation, 120–24
   letter, 121
   request letter, 212, 213, 214, 215
   table of laws, 123

Human Animal Bond Research Initiative Foundation, 187

identification, 110, 115, 196, 201

ignore, 153

iK9, 184

Individualized Education Program, 233

Individualized Education Program (IEP), 118

Individuals with Disabilities Education Act (IDEA), 118, 233

information cards, 149–51

Instagram, 135

intelligent disobedience, 234

interfering with a service dog team, 120

International Association of Assistance Dog Parnters (IAADP), 234

International Association of Assistance Dog Partners (IAADP), *85*, 92, 137

interruption, 27

interruption (task), 28

Job Accommodation Network (JAN), 43, 119, 139

K9's in Special Service, *18*

Kelly and Isaac, 17

laws. *See also* individual laws
   changes to, 188
   federal vs state, 107
   reporting violations, 126
   table of, 108

leave it, 153

letter
  flying, 125, 216
  housing accommodation,
    121, 212, 213, 214, 215
  tips for medical
    professionals, 222
  workplace accommodation,
    218, 219
liability waiver, 102
light guide work, 234
light mobility, 234
Lindsay and Grace, 22
luring, 99
major life activities, 9, 112
major life activity, 234
manners, 63, 83, 87
medical alert dog, 234
medical response dog, 234
Michel and Bobo, 20
Michigan State University
College of Law, 120, 140
Minimum Training
Standards for Public Access,
85, 92, 137
mixed breeds, 74
momentum pull (task), 235
Morris, Veronica, 156
movie theaters, 177
nonprofit status, 49
obedience, basic, 63, 83, 86
obtaining a service dog, 13–
15
  from a program, 45–60
Orthopedic Foundation for
Animals (OFA), 75
owner training

how long, 63
myths, 65
overview, 14
preparation, 66
pros and cons, 61
selecting a prospect, 70
steps, 62–64
parks, 178
Patriot Rovers, 21
PennHIP, 75
personal interview, 55, 58
pet-friendly, 66, 86, 88, 172
petting, unwanted, 153
positive reinforcement, 97,
99
prescription, 109, 117
private lessons, 104
professional trainer, 89
  credentials, 100
  evaluating, 96–101
  finding, 95
professional trainer, 70
programs, 14
  applying, 52–60
  evaluating, 50–52
  finding, 50
  obtaining from, 45–60
  pros and cons, 45
  questions to ask, 56
proofing, 235
prospect, 235
  breed selection, 71–75
  obtaining, 68
  puppy vs adult, 69
protection training, 32

Psychiatric Service Dog Partners (PSDP), 85, 92, 136, 156, 188, 235

Psychiatric Service Dogs Facebook group, 133

public access laws, 66, 114–17, 195

public access skills, 63, 66, 83, 88

public access test (PAT), 84, 85, 92, 116, 235

public restrooms, 165

public transportation, 165

Purdue University Veterinary College, 187

Purina Breed Selector, 75

qualifying for a service dog, 6, 16, 26, 111–14

reasonable accommodation, 119, 120, 139, 208, 235

registration, 5, 7, 109, 120, 203, 204

Rehabilitation Act of 1973. *See* Section 504

religious entity, 117, 178, 208, 236

rental cars, 170

reporting violations, 126

restaurants, 176, 196, 201

reward training. *See* positive reinforcement

school, 118

Section 504, 117, 118, 120, 208, 235, 236

Service Dog Central, 139

Service Dog Gearaholics Facebook group, 133

Service Dog Organization and Trainer Reviews Facebook group, 133

service dog organizations, 136–39, *See also* programs

Service Dog Organizations and Trainer Reviews Facebook group, 51

Service Dogs for Invisible Disabilities Facebook group, 132

shaping, 99

signaling, 27

social considerations, 15, 26, 43, 73
   friends and family, 41–43
socialization, 83, 85, 99
   how to, 144–46
stairs, 163

standards, 85, 92, 137, 138

started dog, 70

state laws, 120

sterile environments, 116, 174, 195

task (vs work), 236

task list, developing, 39

task shopping, 39, 236

tasks, 4, 10
   for agoraphobia, 31
   for anxiety, 30
   for depression, 32
   for dissociation, 32
   for fear of intruders, 32
   for hallucinations, 33
   for impaired memory, 33
   for medication side effects, 33

for nightmares, 34
for racing thoughts, 35
for repetitive/compulsive
behaviors, 35
for self-harm, 35
for sensory overload, 36
for suicidal ideation, 36
number required, 114
starting training, 63
tax deductions, 128–29

taxis, 169

team training, 56

*Teamwork II: A Dog
Training Manual for People
with Disabilities*, 89

Teamwork, Book 1, 87

temperament, 14

temperament testing, 75–81

theft, avoiding, 164

therapy dog, 11, 200, 236

three-way service dog teams,
38

trainer. *See* professional
trainer

training log, 90

training styles, 97

trains, 169

TTY, 236

U.S. Defense Advanced
Research Project Agency
(DARPA), 184

U.S. Department of Labor's
Office of Disability
Employment Policy (ODEP),
139

U.S. Veterans Administration
(VA), 186, 208

Uber, 170

Until Tuesday, 5

vesting, 110, 151, 201

Volhard Puppy Aptitude Test,
77

washing out, 13, 52, 67

whale eye, 236

WordPress, 135

work (vs task), 236

work vs. task, 40

workplace accommodation
letter, 218, 219

workplace environment, 43,
118–19

YouTube, 134

zoos, 116, 206

About the Author

Anne Martinez thrives on providing tools and information to help people explore and achieve their personal goals. Her latest book, *Saved by the Dog: Unleashing Potential with Psychiatric Service Dogs*, combines extensive research and personal experience into an interesting and practical read. Her previous books include *Medical Transcription for Dummies, Get Certified & Get Ahead* (3 editions), and *Cheap Web Tricks: How to Build and Promote a Successful Website without Spending a Dime.* She lives in North Carolina with her service dog, Maisy.

Made in United States
Orlando, FL
13 August 2022

20969780R00143